THE
SERVANT
WHO RULES

Also by Ray C. Stedman

Adventuring Through the Bible
Authentic Christianity
Body Life
God's Final Word
God's Loving Word
Is This All There Is to Life?
Our Riches in Christ
Spiritual Warfare
Talking with My Father
Waiting for the Second Coming

Discovery House Publishers

Books, music, and videos that feed the soul with the Word of God

Box 3566 Grand Rapids, MI 49501

THE
SERVANT
WHO RULES

RAY STEDMAN

EDITED BY JAMES DENNEY

Discovery House Publishers is affiliated with RBC Ministries, Grand
Rapids, Michigan 49512.

Discovery House books are distributed to the trade exclusively by
Barbour Publishing, Inc., Uhrichsville, Ohio 44683.

Book Design: Sherri L. Hoffman

Unless otherwise indicated, Scripture references are from the New
International Version, © 1973, 1978, 1984 by International Bible
Society. Used by permission.

Library of Congress Cataloging-in-Publication Data

Stedman, Ray C.
  [Servant who rules]
  The servant who rules : exploring the gospel of Mark / by Ray C.
Stedman.
    p. cm.
  Originally published: The servant who rules. Waco, Tex.: Word
Books, c1976.
    ISBN 1-57293-084-5
  1. Bible. N.T. Mark I-VIII—Commentaries.   I. Title.

BS2585.3 .S75 2002
226.3'07—dc21
                                                        2001053895

Printed in the United States of America
03 04 05 06 07 08 09 /DP/ 9 8 7 6 5 4 3 2

Contents

Foreword

An author I read many years ago drew a distinction between those who manufacture servanthood and those who distribute it.

"Manufacturers" derive their motivation to serve from within themselves. They serve because they pity the needy or because they believe they have a duty to give something back to the world (noblesse oblige). Some have a compulsive need to be needed; others serve out of guilt and fear. In any case, "manufacturers" soon find their efforts dreary and empty, and they lose interest; for, as Ray Stedman continues to remind us, "the flesh [human endeavor] counts for nothing" (John 6:63).

"Distributors," on the other hand, serve out of an intimate connection to Jesus. They sit at His feet, listen to His words, learn from His great heart, respond to Him in prayer, drink in His love, draw on His power, and distribute His compassion to others. That's what keeps Jesus' servants going for the long haul. They give away all that He has given to them, a concept Ray weaves through the warp and woof of these studies.

It was my privilege to gather weekly with staff members at Peninsula Bible Church when Ray was first thinking his way through the gospel of Mark in preparation for preaching this material, and then I heard each text taught on subsequent Sundays. More importantly, I saw the texts lived out in Ray's life, for he was truly a leader who served over the long haul. He was my friend and teacher for many years, and I sorely miss him. But like Abel, though now in God's presence, he "still speaks."

David Roper
Boise, Idaho

one

The Place to Begin

➤ **Mark 1:1–8**

According to the Wycliffe Bible translators, more than two thousand language groups in the world still do not have any portion of the Bible translated into their language. Those groups are found throughout the world—in Europe, Asia, Africa, the Pacific Islands, and the Americas. Some of these language groups are small; for example, the Dia language is spoken by no more than 1,880 people in a remote section of Papua New Guinea.

I once spent two weeks in Mexico, observing the work of Wycliffe Bible translators. While I was there, I learned that the gospel of Mark is the most widely translated book in the Bible. Almost all Wycliffe translators begin with Mark when they translate the Scriptures into a new language.

Why?

For one thing, it's the shortest of the four gospels, which makes the task of translation shorter and easier. But the brevity of Mark is not the only reason it is so widely translated.

I suspect that an even more important reason is the fact that Mark is an excellent introduction to the gospel story for people of all backgrounds, tribes, and classes. Of the four gospels, Mark is the truly multicultural gospel. It is intended for an international, multiethnic audience. By contrast, the gospel of Matthew is written for Jewish people. That is why Matthew is so rich in Old Testament traditions and Jewish customs. Mark, however, was written for the cosmopolitan Roman world, for people who had no background in the Old Testament. Of the four gospels, Mark is the most easily understood by any audience.

Many scholars think that the gospel of Mark was the earliest book of the New Testament. It was probably written sometime during the A.D. 60s. Scholars differ on whether Mark was written before Matthew or Matthew before Mark, because it is hard to tell who borrowed from whom. We also know that almost the entire gospel of Mark is reproduced in Matthew and Luke (with the exception of a few verses), so it is clear that somebody borrowed from somebody else. But whether Matthew had a copy of Mark's account in front of him as he wrote, or vice versa, nobody knows.

The Author of the Gospel of Mark

We do know that this gospel was written by a young man named John Mark, who figures prominently in the New Testament. His mother was named Mary, and she was a wealthy woman who owned a large house in Jerusalem. In Acts 12, we see that a large group of the early disciples gathered in Mary's house to pray for Peter's release from prison.

Later in Acts, we see that John Mark accompanied Paul and Barnabas on their first missionary journey. For some reason, Mark turned back at the city of Perga and returned to his mother's home instead of continuing with Paul and Barnabas to Asia Minor (modern Turkey). Perhaps Mark was afraid of the robbers that awaited unwary travelers in the Pamphylian mountains. Paul was profoundly disappointed in John Mark, evidently labeling him as a quitter.

Later Paul and Barnabas were preparing for another missionary journey, and John Mark became the cause of an argument between them. Barnabas wanted to take John Mark with them. Paul refused because John Mark "had deserted them in Pamphylia and had not continued with them in the work" (Acts 15:38). The disagreement between Paul and Barnabas was so severe that they parted company. Barnabas took Mark with him to Cyprus, and Paul selected a new companion, Silas, and set off north along the Mediterranean coast.

After this, John Mark dropped out of sight for a time. The next we hear of him, John Mark was an associate of Peter. The apostle Peter spoke affectionately of this young man, calling him "my son Mark" (1 Peter 5:13). Perhaps Peter, who failed Jesus and was restored, understood something that Paul didn't: A person who has failed can learn and grow from failure and become even more valuable to God than someone who has never failed.

Eusebius, a church father writing in the third century A.D., says that the early Christians were so moved and challenged by the stories Peter told them of his time with Christ that they asked Peter's companion, John Mark, to write them down as Peter told them. Perhaps that is how we got the gospel according to Mark. As you read it, you see that Peter figures greatly in the story, and it is easy to imagine that this gospel might reflect Peter's memories of Jesus.

Another possibility is intriguing to speculate on, although it is nothing more than speculation. There is a scene in the Garden of Gethsemane that only Mark records. It takes place during the betrayal and arrest of Jesus.

Then everyone deserted him [Jesus] and fled.
A young man, wearing nothing but a linen garment,

*was following Jesus. When they seized him, he fled naked,
leaving his garment behind.* (MARK 14:50–52)

This unnamed young man stayed behind, following Jesus even
after the other disciples ran away in terror. The soldiers who
arrested Jesus tried to seize this young man, but when they grabbed
for him, the simple linen cloth he wore came away in their hands.
So the anonymous young man ran naked into the night.

Some Bible scholars suggest that this young man was none
other than Mark, the author of this gospel. Perhaps, because of
his fascination with Jesus, he had been hanging around the
fringes of the Lord's disciples, hoping to learn more. The fact
that Mark is the only gospel writer who records this incident
suggests that the young man may well have been Mark.

Another fascinating story, found in Mark 10, is also recorded
in Matthew and Luke—the story of the rich young ruler. It is the
story of a young man who, not long before Jesus was crucified,
came to Him with a question. He was a wealthy member of the
ruling class, an aristocratic young man of culture and refine-
ment. He went up to Jesus, knelt at His feet, and said, "Good
teacher, what must I do to inherit eternal life?"

"Why do you call me good?" replied Jesus. "No one is good—
except God alone. You know the commandments: 'Do not murder, do not commit adultery, do not steal, do not give false
testimony, do not defraud, honor your father and mother.'"

"Teacher," the young ruler answered, "all these I have kept
since I was a boy."

Then Mark records something that neither of the other
accounts tells us: "Jesus looked at him and loved him." That personal note, together with the fact that Mark's mother was a wealthy
woman with a large house in Jerusalem, suggests to me that Mark

may have been that rich young ruler. If this is so, then perhaps the story of the young man who followed Jesus but fled without his clothes is Mark's way of telling us that the rich young ruler reconsidered what Jesus told him and ended up following the Lord. The Scriptures do not explicitly say so, but I strongly suspect it is true.

The Two Halves of Mark

If my speculation is correct—if the author of the gospel of Mark is personally connected with the events he recorded—then that would explain a great deal. For example, it would explain Mark's apparent fascination with two qualities of Jesus that he presents to us in the first verse: "The beginning of the gospel about Jesus Christ, the Son of God."

This is a profound statement. Jesus of Nazareth—the human Jesus, the carpenter—is also the Son of God. The fact that Jesus is man and God made a strong impression on Mark. In fact, the book, organized according to these two qualities of Jesus, easily divides into two halves.

Part 1 of the gospel of Mark consists of Mark 1:1–8:26. The theme of part 1 is The Servant Who Rules, and that section deals with Jesus, the Servant who has all authority in heaven and earth. The theme of part 2, Mark 8:27–16:20, is The Ruler Who Serves, and that part deals with the servant attitude of the Son of God, the rightful Ruler who comes to suffer and die for our sakes. The gospel of Mark begins with these words:

The beginning of the gospel about Jesus Christ, the Son of God.

> *It is written in Isaiah the prophet:*
> *"I will send my messenger ahead of you,*
>   *who will prepare your way"—*
> *"a voice of one calling in the desert,*

'Prepare the way for the Lord,
make straight paths for him.'"

And so John came, baptizing in the desert region and
preaching a baptism of repentance for the forgiveness of sins.
The whole Judean countryside and all the people of
Jerusalem went out to him. Confessing their sins, they were
baptized by him in the Jordan River. (MARK 1:1–5)

That is an amazing statement! Mark's emphasis from the out-
set is the ministry of John the Baptist. This is what he calls "the
beginning of the gospel." The gospel begins, says Mark, with the
voice of God's messenger calling in the wilderness. This amazingly
successful ministry drew crowds from all around that region.

I have visited the wilderness where John once preached. Our
group drove from Jerusalem down to Jericho, then up the valley
of the Jordan River. That valley is indeed a wilderness, a dreary,
desolate, forbidding spot even today. Through that valley flows
the Jordan, the only water for miles around. On either side of the
river is a parched land rimmed by barren desert mountains.

The people of Jerusalem and Judea left the comforts of their
cities, left their recreations and pleasures, and trekked many
rugged miles to hear this man preach. Some of them had to walk
twenty or thirty miles, yet they went willingly, eagerly, and in
such increasing numbers that Mark says, with only slight exag-
geration, that "the whole Judean countryside and all the people
of Jerusalem went out" to hear him.

What is your image of John the Baptist? Most people picture
him as a rugged preacher who thundered at his hearers with fire,
brimstone, and terrible judgment. But was that how the people of
Judea saw him? If that was the kind of message John preached,
who would have listened? Who would have walked twenty or

thirty miles to be condemned and berated by some wild man from the hills? Nobody goes out of his or her way to be excoriated and flayed, and any preacher with a one-note message of condemnation will not have a following for long.

John did not preach that way. Mark tells us that John's message was the beginning of the gospel: the beginning of the good news of Jesus Christ. Good news, not condemnation, brought the people into the desert to hear John the Baptist. John spoke to a universal need in their lives.

What need is that? The same need is universal among human beings today. It is a syndrome that grips the hearts of people everywhere, in every age. That syndrome consists of three elements that always go together: sin, guilt, and fear. Sin produces guilt, and guilt leads to fear.

The Sin-Guilt-Fear Syndrome

What is sin?

In the most basic sense of the word, sin is nothing but self-centeredness. We commit sins because we are thinking of ourselves, loving ourselves, indulging ourselves, and taking care that no one gets ahead of us. We all struggle with sin and self-centeredness. It is the curse that hangs over the human race. We were made by God to be channels of His grace, reaching out to others with His love. But we have become so twisted in our slavery to sin that when we reach out, it is not to give to others but only to take for ourselves. That is the selfish nature of sin.

And sin always produces guilt, the sense of self-hatred and self-condemnation we feel when we know that in our self-centeredness, we have hurt others, hurt ourselves, and damaged our relationship with God. Guilt destroys our self-respect and makes it impossible for us to live in our own skin.

Guilt is always accompanied by fear, because fear is self-distrust. Fear is a sense of our inability to cope with life. We become afraid of the forces within us that we cannot control, that is, our appetite for selfishness and sin. And we become afraid, knowing we have earned God's condemnation. In the Garden of Eden, Adam and Eve sinned; their sin produced guilt. In their guilt, they went and hid in fear. That has been the story of the human race ever since.

The sin-guilt-fear syndrome produces an inner torment the likes of which there is no equal.

I once visited the shrine of Guadalupe in Mexico City. At that site, during the sixteenth century, the Virgin Mary appeared to an Indian and healed him. The place became a healing shrine, drawing the sick and infirm from all over Latin America. There are rooms stacked with crutches, left behind by people who have thrown them away, convinced that they had been healed at the shrine, as some may have been. But on any day you go there, you can see people walking on their knees, leaving bloodstains on the pavement. They crawl for miles over dirty, rough pavement to get to that shrine. Why? Because they have been told that their physical pain will relieve the spiritual and emotional pain of their guilt and fear. They believe that bloody knees create a clean conscience.

That's superstitious nonsense, isn't it? Of course it is, but no more superstitious and nonsensical than many of our approaches to guilt and fear. We don't crawl on bloody knees. We are too sophisticated for that. No, we crawl on our wallets. We use philanthropy—giving money to charities—as a way of salving the pain of our guilt and fear. I know of many individuals and organizations that have benefited handsomely from the guilt and fear of wealthy sinners.

Then there are those who respond to the sin-guilt-fear syndrome by turning into rigid moralists. They deny the reality of their sinfulness, thinking of themselves as practically perfect while looking down on the great mass of sinners around them. By condemning others, they place themselves on a high moral plane. That is how many Christians deal with the guilt that lurks inside them.

Isn't there some way to get true, lasting relief from the sin-guilt-fear syndrome?

The Fourfold Ministry of John the Baptist

A rumor swept through the city of Jerusalem and the surrounding countryside. A message was being preached in the wilderness—a message of release from sin, guilt, and fear. That rumor called people out of their homes and drove them into the barren, forbidding wilderness of the Jordan River. The people went in search of a strange man with a new message.

Oddly, the man did not explain how this message of hope worked, or why it worked, or where it came from. He simply announced its coming. Yet word spread from mouth to mouth, from city to city, until people streamed out into the desert to find John the Baptist, to hear his message, and to be baptized by him. Why did John's announcement have such drawing power?

Mark answers by focusing on four aspects of John's message and ministry. One, John's ministry was foretold in the Old Testament; the prophets spoke of it. Two, John appeared in a wilderness, according to Old Testament promise. Three, John announced the way to God. Four, John assured people that his message was true by the symbol of baptism. Let's take a closer look at each of these aspects of John's ministry.

First, John's ministry was foretold in the Old Testament. Mark quotes two of the prophets, although he names only one, Isaiah. The statement "I will send my messenger ahead of you, who will prepare your way" is a theme from the prophecy of Malachi, the last book of the Old Testament. Mark does not mention Malachi by name, so some critics of the Bible have claimed that Mark was mistaken and ascribed the words of Malachi to Isaiah. But Mark was not mistaken or ignorant; he wanted to stress what Isaiah said because what Malachi wrote agrees with it.

So Mark combines the two and begins with a word from Malachi: "I [God] will send my messenger [John the Baptist] ahead of you [Messiah, Jesus], who will prepare your way." Then Isaiah comes in: "a voice of one calling in the desert, 'Prepare the way for the Lord, make straight paths for him.'" In accordance with that prophecy, says Mark, "John came, baptizing in the desert region and preaching a baptism of repentance for the forgiveness of sins."

God took this step of sending John out before Jesus because He knew that human hearts needed to be prepared before God and humankind could come together. The Messiah, God in human form, could not just appear and expect to be received. So John was sent to go before the Lord Jesus and prepare the way for Him by means of repentance. We will examine that repentance soon.

Why a Wilderness?

Why was it predetermined that John should begin his ministry in the wilderness? That makes no public relations sense. If you want to make an impact on the population, you have to go where the people are—to the cities, not the wilderness. But God doesn't take advice from public relations experts. He does what human wisdom least expects. So God sent John the Baptist out to the worst possible place for ministry. And it worked.

Why did God choose the wilderness as the starting point for the gospel? Because it is a symbol of where we are as human beings. We are in the wilderness, the desert. John's message went into the wilderness of human sin, folly, and fallenness. The desert is a picture of our dry, empty, barren, weary lives.

How many times have we heard of famous Hollywood couples who supposedly had the ideal marriage, only to hear later of their breakup and divorce because their relationship became boring and empty? If the lives of Hollywood's rich and famous can be dry, empty, barren, and bored, what hope is there for the rest of us? If fame, wealth, travel, and an endless swirl of parties can become a desert existence, then the human condition is a wilderness indeed.

A Christian friend told me about his longtime neighbor, a bright and wealthy man who seemed to have everything going for him. One day this neighbor sat at my friend's kitchen table, buried his face in his hands, and said despairingly, "I am so bored!" Two weeks later he took his life.

That is the desert of human existence. That is where people live. And that is why John went into the wilderness. John's appearance is God's symbol to us of the hope that will spring up, even in the midst of our desert of hopelessness and desperation.

The Meaning of Forgiveness

"And so John came," says Mark, "baptizing in the desert region and preaching a baptism of repentance for the forgiveness of sins." This was an astounding message, a thunderbolt of good news. John's announcement was that human beings come to God by means of repentance, and the result of repentance is the forgiveness of sins. The greatest blessing we can experience is to have our sins forgiven. The people of Judea knew that they were lost in their sins, so when a message of forgiveness thundered forth from the desert, they streamed out of Jerusalem to hear it.

Forgiveness is something few of us understand well. Most of us have grown up with the idea that you forgive people only after they apologize, but that is not biblical forgiveness. Few broken relationships would ever be restored and reconciled if forgiveness began only after an apology had been offered. Biblical forgiveness begins before the offender comes to you with an apology.

We find the perfect model of forgiveness in the story Jesus told of the prodigal son. A prodigal is an ungrateful and careless spendthrift. The prodigal son in the story left his father, went to a far country, spent all that he had received from his father, then returned home broken and humbled, ready to live as a servant in his father's house. But when the father saw the boy, his arms opened wide in love, acceptance, and forgiveness. Before the son could say a word, the father kissed and hugged him and ordered a party in his honor. That's biblical forgiveness, God's forgiveness—forgiveness that is offered before even a single syllable of apology is uttered.

Forgiveness stands ready to forget the hurt, to blot the offense from memory. True forgiveness never brings up the subject again. Biblical forgiveness treats the offender as if the offense had never happened. The basis for God's forgiveness is the cross of Jesus Christ. The cross enables God to forgive us because it maintains His justice. But the basis on which we are called to forgive is different. Our basis for forgiving others is the fact that we have been forgiven.

That is why Jesus told the story of the man who had been forgiven a tremendous debt. After being forgiven, that man went to another man who owed him a paltry sum, grabbed him by the throat, and demanded, "Pay back what you owe me!" (Matthew 18:28). That, Jesus says, is what we are like when we do not forgive those who offend us. We have been forgiven a huge debt, and on that basis we are to forgive others. Forgiveness begins with a change of attitude in the heart of the one offended.

But forgiveness can never be complete until there has been a change of heart in the offender. It is not enough for forgiveness to be offered; forgiveness must also be accepted. The offender must acknowledge guilt and remorse. That is the repentance John the Baptist talks about. The offender must change his or her mind about the offense, stop justifying it, and admit he or she has been hurtful and wrong. Only then can the forgiveness that was offered be received.

John came preaching repentance because the place of repentance is where God meets humanity.

God's Bulldozer

The Old Testament prophet Isaiah predicted that the message of John the Baptist would be like a great bulldozer, building a highway in the desert so that God would be able to come reach isolated human souls in the midst of the wilderness. "Every valley shall be raised up," says Isaiah 40:4, "every mountain and hill made low; the rough ground shall become level, the rugged places a plain." Without a road, you cannot drive out into the desert to help those who are wandering and lost. So John was the highway builder who made a path in the desert with the message of repentance and forgiveness.

Repentance is the great leveler. It fills in the valleys and depressed places of our lives—the places where we beat ourselves down and torture ourselves with guilt—and lifts them up. It also brings down all the high peaks of pride that we stand on when we refuse to admit we are wrong. Repentance takes the crooked places, where we have lied and deceived, and straightens them out. And it makes the rough places of our lives plain and smooth. Isn't that beautiful imagery to describe the role of repentance in our lives?

Mark goes on to describe the appearance of John the Baptist:

> *John wore clothing made of camel's hair, with a leather belt around his waist, and he ate locusts and wild honey.*
>
> (MARK 1:6)

Why does Mark include these details? The rugged prophet John was no fashion plate, with his camel's hair clothes, leather sandals, and leather girdle around his waist—all very much like the Old Testament prophet Elijah. John's diet was simple: locusts (grasshoppers) and wild honey. These details are important, or they would not have been included. They are symbolic of an important truth. But what do they symbolize?

Above all, these details suggest simplicity. You cannot wear any more simple clothing, or eat a more basic diet, than John the Baptist did. These details are representative of his ministry, which was one of simple beginnings. This is the beginning of the gospel of Jesus Christ, and it begins with a simple man preaching a simple message of repentance, heralding the coming of the Son of God.

John's diet, by the way, was balanced. Grasshoppers are protein, and honey is carbohydrate. John's diet was in beautiful balance, so he was a healthy man. But it was an elementary, rudimentary sort of diet, just as his ministry was elementary, rudimentary, and simple.

It is important to see that, as John states, his ministry was incomplete.

> This was his message: "After me will come one more powerful than I, the thongs of whose sandals I am not worthy to stoop down and untie. I baptize you with water, but he will baptize you with the Holy Spirit." (MARK 1:7–8)

John is honest and humble. He says, in effect, "Don't look to me for answers beyond what I have already told you about repentance. Anything beyond that must come from another, who is coming right after me. He is so far above me and beyond me that I am not even worthy to untie His shoes. The sign of His greatness is that, although I can baptize you with a baptism of outer cleansing, He will cleanse you inwardly with the Spirit of God" (see Matthew 3:11; John 1:15).

John is saying that he could bring people to God, but he could not lead them into a daily experience of life in the Spirit of God. Only Jesus could impart the life of the Spirit. John came to announce that Jesus was coming. And when Jesus came, He would baptize people with the Holy Spirit so that they could live, day by day, in the transforming life of God.

So much of Christian preaching today is on the same order as John's ministry. It is incomplete, designed only to bring people to God and nothing more. The message often stops at the point of the initial decision, and people are not taught how to live beyond that point. They have John's baptism, but they have never been baptized with the Spirit of God, with the reality of Christian living that is to come after John.

John the Baptist brought people to Christ by the only way anyone can come: acknowledgment of sin and guilt. When people come this way, God meets them, cleanses them, and forgives them. John demonstrated this truth by the baptism he performed. But there is a greater baptism, and that is the baptism of the Holy Spirit. On the Day of Pentecost, the seventh Sunday after Easter, the apostle Peter stood and offered two things to the people: forgiveness of sins and the promise of the Spirit. God still offers His forgiveness and His Spirit to every person who will begin at the beginning, that is, the place of repentance.

The Place of Repentance

Have you repented? Have you changed your mind, stopped defending yourself, stopped blaming others for your failures and sins? Have you said, "I have no excuses, no scapegoats, no one else to blame, Lord. The sin is all mine, the guilt is all mine, and only you can take it away"? That is the place of repentance. That is the place where God will meet you. At the place of repentance, He washes away our guilt, cleanses us from sin, and forgives. If you have never repented, I urge you to do so now. In the quiet of your heart, where God alone hears, say to Him, "Lord, I repent. Send me the Holy Spirit through Jesus the Lord."

And He will.

If you are a Christian with a desert area in your life and you can't find your way out of it, this is the place to begin. Repent, acknowledge the emptiness and barrenness of your life, and God will meet you there and wash it all away. He does not have a word of condemnation for you, just a word of cleansing—if you meet Him at that place of repentance.

two

Jesus Came

> ➤ **Mark 1:9–15**

The grandfather entered the child's bedroom. A wide grin brightened his kind, warm face. "Davy!" he said, spreading his arms for a hug.

"Grampa!" shrieked the delighted two-year-old from his playpen. "Grampa, hug!"

"Sure, I'll give you a hug, Davy," said the grandfather. And with that, the old man reached out to his grandson and scooped him up out of the playpen, snuggling the boy in his strong arms. After a big hug, the grandfather set the boy down outside the playpen, among his Fisher-Price® toys, and they began to play together.

Minutes later, the boy's mother walked into the room. "Davy!" she said sternly. "You know I put you in the playpen because you've been naughty! You shouldn't have told Grampa to take you out!"

Davy's eyes puddled up, and he began to cry. The grandfather instantly felt terrible. He didn't know that his grandson had been given a time out in the playpen as a punishment. Now he had made a bad situation even worse for his little grandson.

"Grampa, play with me!" the boy said in pitiful voice that broke the old man's heart.

But the mother was unbending. "Davy, you know you have to go back into the playpen." She lifted the boy up and put him back in solitary confinement. The boy wailed in despair.

What could the grandfather do? He knew he couldn't overrule the boy's mother. But his heart went out to the poor boy.

Then the grandfather had an idea.

"Dad!" said the mother. "What do you think you're doing?"

"The only thing I can do," said the grandfather as he climbed into the playpen with his grandson. The child was being punished, and rightfully so. The only way the grandfather could show mercy to the boy was by descending to Davy's situation and taking Davy's punishment onto himself.

And that is what happened in your life and in mine the day Jesus came.

Jesus walked into the wilderness of our lives, becoming one with us, accepting the restrictions of life in human form, accepting our punishment, and suffering our pain. Jesus came so that we could have life—abundant life. In Mark 1:9, we read,

> *At that time Jesus came from Nazareth in Galilee and was baptized by John in the Jordan.*

Note those two little words near the beginning of that verse: "Jesus came." Those words are a formula for dramatic, radical change.

In the next two paragraphs, Mark 1:9–15, the phrase "Jesus came" occurs twice. "At that time Jesus came from Nazareth in Galilee" (Mark 1:9). "Now after John was arrested, Jesus came into Galilee, preaching the gospel of God" (Mark 1:14 RSV). Mark says that when Jesus came, He came in this twofold way. Verse 9 begins the record of the baptism and temptation of Jesus. Jesus came, He was baptized, and He was tempted, says Mark. Mark puts the latter two in the passive voice; that is, baptism and temptation were acts done to Jesus. This indicates that they were acts in preparation for His ministry.

After that, says verse 14, Jesus came into Galilee preaching. In that one word, we see the activity that marked the career of Jesus: He came preaching.

Let us look at the two acts of preparation Mark records at the beginning of the ministry of the Lord Jesus.

> *At that time Jesus came from Nazareth in Galilee and was baptized by John in the Jordan. As Jesus was coming up out of the water, he saw heaven being torn open and the Spirit descending on him like a dove. And a voice came from heaven: "You are my Son, whom I love; with you I am well pleased."* (MARK 1:9–11)

All four gospels record the baptism of Jesus, so the importance of this event in the life of our Lord is underscored. Yet there is something strange about this baptism.

Notice the context of this event. A remarkable spiritual awakening has broken out in Israel. Literally thousands of people have left homes, jobs, and families. Crowds stream from the cities and into the desert to hear the preaching of a strange, rugged prophet, John the Baptist. John baptizes all who repent and seek forgiveness. That is the emphasis of John's ministry. He baptizes as a sign of God's cleansing on the confession of sin and guilt.

But something strange happens when Jesus comes out of Galilee to be baptized by John. When Jesus presents Himself for baptism, John protests. In Matthew's account of Jesus' baptism, we see that John says to the Lord, "I need to be baptized by you, and do you come to me?" (Matthew 3:14). That is a remarkable statement, especially in view of the fact that John did not know at this time that Jesus was the Messiah. In fact, John's account tells us that John the Baptist knew this only when he saw the Spirit of God descending on Jesus and remaining on Him, for that was the sign God had given to John. Only then did John realize that Jesus was the one who was to come, the one he had been announcing (John 1:32–34).

John had known Jesus ever since boyhood, for they were cousins. (And if you can't find fault with your relatives, whom can you fault?) Yet when this relative comes, John says of Him, "You don't need to be baptized. I do! Why are you coming to me?" All the other people who came to John had been baptized on their repentance and confession of sins, but John had never seen any sin in Jesus' life, so there was nothing for Jesus to repent of.

Jesus answered John in a remarkable way, recorded in Matthew 3:15: "Let it be so now; it is proper for us to do this to fulfill all righteousness." Why was Jesus baptized by John the Baptist? In this brief account, Mark suggests three reasons.

Jesus' Baptism: An Act of Identification with Us

First, Jesus' baptism was an act of identification. Jesus associated Himself with us. Like the grandfather we met at the beginning of this chapter, Jesus climbed into our playpen with us. He took our place, not just on the cross but first of all in baptism. This was the first step leading to that moment when He would be made sin for us, when He would become what we are. When He was baptized with a baptism of repentance and confession of sin, even though He was sinless, Jesus willingly took our place as sinners.

I like the way Dr. H. A. Ironside explained this. We are like paupers who have accumulated so many debts that we cannot pay them. These are our sins. These claims are made against us, and we cannot possibly meet them. But when Jesus came, He took all these mortgages and notes and bills we could not pay and He endorsed them with His name—a sign of His intention to pay our debts for us. This is what His baptism signifies. This is why Jesus said to John the Baptist, "It is proper for us to do this to fulfill all righteousness." Jesus declared His intention to meet the righteous demands of God by undertaking to pay all our debts. So the baptism was an act of identification with us.

Jesus' Baptism: An Empowering Moment

Second, Jesus' baptism was an empowering moment. Mark writes, "As Jesus was coming up out of the water, he saw heaven being torn open and the Spirit descending on him like a dove. And a voice came from heaven: 'You are my Son, whom I love; with you I am well pleased'" (Mark 1:10–11). It is significant that at the moment Jesus begins to take our place, the Father gives Him the gift of the Holy Spirit. There is no greater gift God can give than the gift of His Spirit.

This is not the first time Jesus had the Spirit. We must not think of it that way. The Bible tells us that John the Baptist was filled with the Holy Spirit from his mother's womb. And if that was true of John, it was true of Jesus. Our Lord lived by the Spirit during those quiet years in Nazareth. He submitted to His parents, grew up in a carpenter's shop, and learned the trade. Through those uneventful days, living in ordinary circumstances in that little village, Jesus lived by the power of the Spirit in His life. There is no question about it.

What happens, then, when the Spirit comes on Jesus like a dove? He is given a new manifestation of the Spirit, especially in terms of power. To use the language of Scripture, Jesus was anointed by the Spirit at this point. In Old Testament times, kings and priests were anointed for office in a solemn ceremony that involved pouring oil on their heads. This is the picture of what now occurs in Jesus' life. God, through the Spirit, anoints Jesus with power to meet the demands of His coming ministry. The Spirit is always associated with the coming of power into a human life.

Luke tells us that some weeks after our Lord is anointed with power by the Holy Spirit, He goes to the synagogue at Nazareth, stands before the congregation, and reads Isaiah 61:1–2, a passage He applies to Himself:

> *"The Spirit of the Lord is on me,*
> *because he has anointed me*
> *to preach good news to the poor.*
> *He has sent me to proclaim freedom for the prisoners*
> *and recovery of sight for the blind,*
> *to release the oppressed,*
> *to proclaim the year of the Lord's favor."* (LUKE 4:18–19)

If you look over the three-and-a-half-year span of Jesus' ministry that follows, you see that this passage from Isaiah precisely describes what Jesus was about to do. His public ministry was beginning, and it began with the anointing power of the Holy Spirit.

Do not think of God's anointing as something remote from your experience. God also anoints ordinary human beings like you and me with the power of His Spirit. That is the thrust of our Lord's teaching. Jesus took our place; therefore, what happened to Him can and must happen in us.

That is why Jesus, standing with His disciples after the resurrection, said to them, "You will receive power when the Holy Spirit comes on you; and you will be my witnesses in Jerusalem, and in all Judea and Samaria, and to the ends of the earth" (Acts 1:8). Amazing thought! The Spirit of God must come on us. The gift of the Holy Spirit must be given to us so that we can live as God wants us to live.

Why does God anoint us with His Spirit of power? Not for us to use performing, dramatic, showy acts that bring glory to ourselves. No, God gives us His Spirit so that we can experience a new quality of life, a life that is irresistible in its beauty and attraction, yet at the same time quiet and gentle. The symbol God uses to display this new kind of power is significant: a dove.

Why did God choose a dove? Football teams use birds of prey as emblems of power, strength, and aggression. The National Football League includes such teams as the Atlanta Falcons, the Baltimore Ravens, the Seattle Seahawks, and the Philadelphia Eagles—all fierce and regal predators. But no football team would ever call itself the Doves.

In Matthew 10:16, Jesus talks about being "as innocent as doves." A dove is a gentle bird that does not resist, does not fight back, and yet is irresistible. That is the new kind of power Jesus describes—the power of love. Love can be beaten and battered, tortured, and put to death, yet it will rise again and win the day. That is the power Jesus came to model for us and release in us. It is the greatest force in the world, yet it does not intimidate or destroy. Love only attracts and heals.

As Christians, we are not called to seek power and dominance over others; instead, we must seek humility. "The greatest among you will be your servant," said Jesus (Matthew 23:11). And Peter put it this way: "Humble yourselves, therefore, under God's mighty hand, that he may lift you up in due time" (1 Peter 5:6). Humility brings all of the power of God into our lives; pride makes God our enemy.

Jesus' Baptism: A Sign of Assurance

Third, Jesus' baptism was a sign of assurance. There came a voice from heaven: "You are my Son, whom I love; with you I am well pleased" (Mark 1:11). In Matthew it is stated a little differently: "This is my Son, whom I love; with him I am well pleased" (Matthew 3:17). This was said as a testimony to those who were watching the scene. But Mark 1:11 and Luke 3:22 report that the voice addresses Jesus, saying, "You are my Son, whom I love." There have been quarrels among various Bible scholars and critics over which version is correct, and those quarrels show how little we understand the ways of God.

I believe both versions are right. Those who stood nearby heard the voice say, "This is my Son," which was God's stamp of approval on the thirty years Jesus had spent in Nazareth, those quiet years of Jesus' life about which Scripture is silent. Some people have wondered, "Wasn't Jesus a sinner like everyone else? As a child, wasn't He sometimes disobedient or rebellious? He didn't live a perfect life as a boy! Who knows what kind of trouble He got into during those years the Bible doesn't tell us about?" God knew! And His testimony was clear: "This is my Son, whom I love; with him I am well pleased." It was God's testimony to the purity of those years.

But when Jesus heard the voice, it said, "You are my Son, whom I love." These words were addressed directly to Him as a message of assurance and security. We must not think that because Jesus was the Son of God, He was automatically empowered against all obstacles, threats, and fears. He was fully human, as we are. That is what Scripture says. He needed the assurance of the Father's love and approval. He needed a message from the Father, telling Him who He was.

Psychologists tell us that if we do not know who we are, we have little poise and confidence. We have to know who we are before we can be effective and authoritative in our speech and actions. This is what God gave to Jesus at His baptism: the security of knowing His identity as the beloved Son of God.

God now makes this same bold statement about our identity in Him. The amazing good news for you and me as followers of Christ is that God views us just as He viewed Jesus, as His beloved children. As Paul writes, "The Spirit himself testifies with our spirit that we are God's children. Now if we are children, then we are heirs—heirs of God and coheirs with Christ, if indeed we share in his sufferings in order that we may also share in his glory" (Romans 8:16–17). What an amazing statement! Because of our identification with Christ, God says to you and me, "You are my child, whom I love. With you I am well pleased." That is the source of our security and identity.

Jesus began His ministry with a sense of assurance from the Father that all was well in His life. That assurance empowered Him to withstand the first great test of His ministry on earth.

Tested in the Wilderness

The first act of preparation in Jesus' life was baptism. Next Mark shows us the second act of preparation, Jesus' temptation.

> *At once the Spirit sent him out into the desert, and he was*
> *in the desert forty days, being tempted by Satan. He was with*
> *the wild animals, and angels attended him.* (MARK 1:12–13)

Part of Jesus' preparation was the temptation He went through in the desert. Mark records this event, as do Matthew and Luke; John omits it. But it was necessary that our Lord experience this testing. Notice the strong language Mark uses in his brief but powerful narrative. There are three key elements of the story to be understood.

First, the Spirit immediately ("at once") sent Jesus out into the wilderness. The meaning of the original language is that the Spirit drove Jesus into the wilderness. That means Jesus felt a strong inner compulsion, a powerful urge to go into the wilderness and face the tempter on his own ground.

I vividly recall my first high school football practice. It was something I felt eager to do, something I felt I had to do to prove my manhood. Yet I was also a bit scared and anxious. I didn't know what football would do to me. Would I measure up? Would I perform well? Would I get injured? Although I was inwardly concerned, I would not admit my fears. Although I was afraid, I was still eager to jump into the game and prove myself.

I suspect that this is a faint glimmer of the feelings Jesus faced as He approached His testing in the desert. He felt a strong inner urging to prove His manhood before taking on the ultimate test at the cross of Calvary. He had to be tempted and tested for His sake. He did not dare go out to a ministry while He was yet untried. In order to know what was in Himself—what He could and could not stand—He was driven by the Spirit to this lonely place. This was intended to toughen Him. This is what God always does with His own. He toughens them by driving them out into these kinds of experiences.

In the wilderness, Jesus went through forty days of hunger, thirst, and deprivation. Forty days is a long time to go without food. I have sometimes fasted for as long as three days and have found it endurable. For a day or two, hunger increases; then, after a while, it fades. But wait a while longer, and it returns in an intensified form. Imagine forty days without food. Take out a calendar and count back forty days. Think of what you were doing forty days ago. It seems like ancient history, doesn't it? Now imagine you have not eaten one bite in all that time.

Reading carefully, we see that Mark suggests something that we don't find in the other gospel accounts. Throughout that forty-day period, the devil was there at Jesus' side, trying to break Him, coming at Him with every means of attack at his disposal. Satan attacked Jesus in His body, soul, and spirit. He probed and assaulted and sifted Jesus. He bombarded Jesus with every thought and temptation human beings are subject to. The accounts in Matthew and Luke gather up only the final temptations, the final horrific tests that Satan gave to Jesus. But Mark suggests that Satan was tormenting and testing Jesus throughout the forty-day period.

Most of us would have found the physical hunger by itself to be unendurable. One wonders if Jesus knew, when He went out into the wilderness, that He would be there for forty days. In any case, He expected that God would supply His needs. Yet His privation went on, week after week, while His body grew weaker and weaker. The tempter would come and say, "God doesn't care for you anymore. He's abandoned you. You say you're the Son of God? Why, He's made no provision for you!" After days of such attacks, the tempter would make a subtle suggestion: "If you are the Son of God, why don't you turn the stones into bread?" (see Matthew 4:3; Luke 4:3). That is how Satan works. He comes to us in our low points, when we wonder if God is there, when we are discouraged, defeated, depressed. At those low points in our lives, Satan offers us a way to be comforted. But that is not God's way to comfort; it is the path of sin, leading to guilt and destruction. That was the temptation Jesus faced.

Then imagine the loneliness Jesus felt after forty days without human companionship. Such isolation can tempt a man to want to prove himself before masses of people and even to seek their admiration. In the depths of His loneliness, the tempter came and set Jesus on a high pinnacle of the temple and told Him to cast Himself down. Matthew records:

> *Then the devil took him to the holy city and had him stand on the highest point of the temple. "If you are the Son of God," he said, "throw yourself down. For it is written:*
>
> *"'He will command his angels concerning you, and they will lift you up in their hands, so that you will not strike your foot against a stone.'"*
> (MATTHEW 4:5–6)

Here Satan quotes Psalm 91:11–12 and suggests, "People will follow you, Jesus, when they see God support you and sustain you in this supernatural way." And don't think Jesus wasn't tempted. He was! Here was an opportunity to gain the approval of the masses by the exercise of power apart from the will of God. And aren't we all tempted that way? I have been. I'm sure you have too.

Then comes the last temptation. As Jesus reaches the depth of His torture and vulnerability, the devil suggests a way Jesus can gain what He wants without having to go through the crucifixion. He takes Jesus to a high mountain and shows Him all the kingdoms of the world. This is Jesus' goal: to come into His kingdom and rule it as the Messiah. God's plan would take Jesus to His goal, but only after He had passed through the shadow of the cross. Satan's plan is a shortcut, a way to circumvent the cross. Satan's offer to Jesus is simple and compelling: "All this I will give you," he said, "if you will bow down and worship me" (Matthew 4:9).

Jesus is our example in times of temptation. He answered temptation in the same way that we are to answer: by simple reliance on God's Word. Three times Jesus answered Satan with the words "it is written." In Matthew 4, we read:

Jesus answered, "It is written: 'Man does not live on bread alone, but on every word that comes from the mouth of God.'" (MATTHEW 4:4; Jesus quoted Deuteronomy 8:3)

Jesus answered him, "It is also written: 'Do not put the Lord your God to the test.'" (MATTHEW 4:7; Jesus quoted Deuteronomy 6:16)

Jesus said to him, "Away from me, Satan! For it is written: 'Worship the Lord your God, and serve him only.'" (MATTHEW 4:10; Jesus quoted DEUTERONOMY 6:13)

Three times Jesus answered the devil with Scripture. In times of physical, mental, and spiritual torment and temptation, our emotions will rise and fall, but the Word of God stands firm. It is written. It stands written. It is changeless and sure. God's Word is our rock when we are under satanic attack.

You may ask why God allows temptation to come into our lives. When we are tempted, we are tested. God allows us to be tempted and tested so that we can be toughened and strengthened. Many years ago, I came across a poem that powerfully expresses what God is doing in our lives through times of testing:

> When God wants to drill a man,
> And thrill a man,
> And skill a man;
> When God wants to mold a man
> To play the noblest part,
> When He yearns with all His heart
> To create so great and bold a man
> That all the world shall be amazed,
> Watch His methods, watch His ways—

How He ruthlessly perfects
Whom He royally elects.
How He hammers him and hurts him,
And with mighty blows, converts him
Into trial shapes of clay
Which only God understands,
While his tortured heart is crying,
And he lifts beseeching hands.
How He bends but never breaks
When His good He undertakes.
How He uses
Whom He chooses,
And with every purpose, fuses him,
By every act, induces him
To try His splendor out.
God knows what He's about.

—DALE MARTIN STONE

It's true. God knows what He's about during times of temptation and testing in our lives, just as He knew what He was about during the temptation of His Son.

Attended by Beasts and Angels

Mark records one other thing about Jesus' temptation. Let's take another look at Mark's brief but eloquent account of that wilderness experience.

> At once the Spirit sent him out into the desert, and he was in the desert forty days, being tempted by Satan. He was with the wild animals, and angels attended him.
>
> (MARK 1:12–13)

Jesus had no human companionship or help. The only voice He heard in the wilderness was the voice of the enemy. Yet He was not alone. He was sustained by a ministry of comfort that came in unusual ways. He was with the wild animals, and the angels came and ministered to Him. What picture enters your mind when you imagine Jesus in the wilderness, surrounded by wild animals? Do you suppose that Jesus was afraid of being attacked by them? The beasts of that wilderness probably included leopards, lions, bears, and other carnivores. But all beasts are gentle beasts in the presence of the one who created them. They were His companions. They comforted Him and helped Him. I can easily picture Jesus, His body thin from hunger and cold from exposure, snuggled up between two mountain lions, being physically ministered to by the wild but friendly beasts.

Further, the angels ministered to Him. That means His thought life was sustained, His emotions were upheld, His mental faculties were kept clear. That is the ministry of angels, creatures who are invisible yet real. Many of us have experienced the ministry of angels without knowing it. When your spirits are suddenly uplifted and you do not know why, that is often the ministry of angels. Jesus was upheld that way.

Preaching of the Kingdom

God had been preparing Jesus for His public ministry. First, Jesus was baptized and equipped by the Spirit. Second, Jesus was toughened and tested in the wilderness. Now we come to a transition point as Jesus enters Galilee to begin His public ministry.

After John was put in prison, Jesus went into Galilee, proclaiming the good news of God. "The time has come," he said.

"The kingdom of God is near. Repent and believe the good news!" (MARK 1:14–15)

Here Mark passes over a full year of Jesus' ministry. The details of that first year are found only in John's account: the miracle at the wedding at Cana, His encounter with Nicodemus, His conversation with the woman at the well, and so forth. Mark passes over all of this, beginning his account of the ministry of Jesus with the calling of the disciples by the Sea of Galilee. But notice two things Mark underscores about Jesus.

First, Jesus came preaching the gospel of God. His method was preaching. I do not think preaching will ever be superseded by anything else, because good preaching is, at its most essential, the revelation of reality. True, honest, biblical preaching allows people to see what life is really about. Paul describes his preaching in 2 Corinthians 4:2: "by setting forth the truth plainly we commend ourselves to every man's conscience in the sight of God." That is true preaching, and that is what Jesus came to do. He came to open the eyes of the people to the true nature of human and spiritual reality.

Second, Jesus' message was, "The kingdom of God is near." What did He mean by "the kingdom of God"? By this phrase, Jesus speaks of the fact that we are surrounded by an invisible spiritual kingdom. From that realm, great forces, evil and good, act on our lives. In that kingdom, Jesus is Lord and reigns supreme. That kingdom governs all the events of history and all the events of our daily lives and circumstances. As citizens of God's kingdom, we are connected to the ultimate force that governs all of reality, from the details of our daily lives to the infinite reaches of time and space.

Jesus came with the good news that all the power of God is now available to break the helpless deadlock into which humanity has fallen. Scripture tells us that in our natural condition, we are helpless. We like to think we can save ourselves and correct our condition, but the truth is that we are hopeless without the merciful intervention of God. The good news that Jesus announced at the beginning of His public ministry is that God's power has broken through, the kingdom of God is at hand, and the King has come. The power of God, through the Holy Spirit, can change lives, taking the worst sinner and transforming him or her into a model of Christlikeness.

That is the kingdom of God. As Paul writes, "The kingdom of God is not a matter of eating and drinking, but of righteousness, peace and joy in the Holy Spirit" (Romans 14:17). God is available and open to all who are willing to acknowledge their need of Him. That is why Jesus said, "Blessed are the poor in spirit, for theirs is the kingdom of heaven" (Matthew 5:3).

Do you want to enter the kingdom of God? Do you want to experience the righteousness, peace, and joy of God? The kingdom of God is near to you. And the place to enter that kingdom is the place of repentance.

three

A Day in the Life of Jesus

➤ Mark 1:16–39

In his semi-autobiographical novel *One Day in the Life of Ivan Denisovich,* Alexander Solzhenitsyn spends roughly 150 pages detailing the miseries and horrors of one day in a Soviet prison camp. Ivan is an innocent man falsely imprisoned, a former Russian soldier who escaped from a Nazi prison camp. On his return to Russia, his government imprisons him for ten years, accusing him of defecting to the Nazis and then coming back as a spy. In blunt, simple language, Solzhenitsyn describes one injustice after another as Ivan and his fellow prisoners try to survive the extreme Siberian cold, the brutality of the guards, the torture and drudgery of the forced labor, and the grinding misery of hunger. The title underscores the fact that this day of unrelenting horrors is just one day of the 3,653 days of Ivan's sentence. At the end of the book, we find that Ivan has survived that day, but we know that tomorrow, the struggle for survival begins all over again. And it will continue, day after day, until the last day of his unjust imprisonment or his death—whichever comes first.

It has become a popular literary technique to create a portrait of a character by tracing the events of one day in that character's life. Solzhenitsyn used this approach effectively, and so did Jim Bishop in such books as *The Day Lincoln Was Shot, The Day Kennedy Was Shot,* and *The Day Christ Died.* As we approach Mark 1:16–39, we see that Mark uses a similar literary approach in his gospel as he traces for us a day in the life of Jesus.

The day begins in the bright sunshine of a Galilean morning when Jesus walks out alongside the lake. Then it moves into a midmorning visit to a synagogue in Capernaum, for this day was a Sabbath day. Then the story proceeds to an afternoon visit at the home of Peter and Andrew. Next it traces the events of a busy evening in that city as thousands gather to be ministered to by Jesus. The account of this day concludes with a solitary midnight prayer vigil in the hills, a vigil that continues through the lonely hours of the early morning. Thus a full twenty-four hours is given to us in this account, assembled from the eyewitness memories Mark had of Jesus, plus the stories Peter had told him.

One theme is apparent as we read the account of this day: the authority of Jesus. Mark sees the authority of Jesus as descending from the servant character of Jesus. This was a radical concept for Mark's era, just as it is a radical idea today. A servant is a person of lowliness, of little or no authority. How could authority arise from the role of being a servant? Yet that principle flows throughout the Old and New Testaments. From the Old Testament story of Joseph, who was enslaved and imprisoned in Egypt, then exalted by God to a position of national leadership, to the New Testament story of Jesus, we see this principle proven again and again: God bestows authority and power on the one who voluntarily serves.

Mark records six marks of Jesus' authority that are revealed on that one day. The first mark of His authority is given to us in Mark 1:16–20.

As Jesus walked beside the Sea of Galilee, he saw Simon and his brother Andrew casting a net into the lake, for they were fishermen. "Come, follow me," Jesus said, "and I will make you fishers of men." At once they left their nets and followed him.

When he had gone a little farther, he saw James son of Zebedee and his brother John in a boat, preparing their nets. Without delay he called them, and they left their father Zebedee in the boat with the hired men and followed him.

This is not the first time Jesus ever saw these men. They were disciples of John the Baptist, and Jesus had met them earlier in Judea. They had even followed Him for a time as His disciples. This is not the story of their first encounter with Jesus but of the day they received their official call to a deeper and continuous level of discipleship. He said to them, "Come, follow me, and I will make you fishers of men." He assumes full responsibility for training them to be effective leaders and ministers of the gospel.

At the moment Jesus calls them, these men are fishers of fish, not fishers of men. They are simple Galilean fishermen, rough, unlearned, governed by passions and prejudices, narrow in their outlook. Before they could become fishers of men, they needed to become universal in their view. They needed to learn how to walk in reliance on the power of the Spirit of God. Jesus assumes the responsibility for molding them into fishers of men.

Whenever Jesus calls us to any task, He assumes responsibility to equip and prepare us for that task. If we follow Him, yield to Him, and cooperate with Him, He will make us useful channels for His blessing, useful agents for His eternal plan.

God's Power and Your Unique Personality

It is instructive to notice the individual character and personality of each man in this story and how the task he is doing as a simple fisherman symbolizes the ministry he will have after Jesus has trained and equipped him. Peter and Andrew were casting their nets into the sea, which symbolizes that they would one day become great evangelists who would throw out spiritual nets and bring in huge hauls of human souls. We see a foreshadowing of how Andrew will lead many people to Christ, even as he brings his brother Peter to meet Christ. And Peter will become a great evangelist on the Day of Pentecost, when three thousand people respond to his gospel and become Christians.

But Mark shows that James and John were not fishing when Jesus called them. Instead, they were preparing their nets (some translations say "mending their nets"). The Greek word for "mending" or "preparing" is the same word that Paul uses when he says that pastors and teachers in the church are "to prepare God's people for works of service, so that the body of Christ may be built up" (Ephesians 4:12). Just as James and John were preparing their nets and getting them ready when Jesus called them, so they were later found to be preparing people for ministry after Jesus had mentored and taught them. When our Lord calls us, He prepares us for service. Yet He does so in such a way as to retain the nuances of personality that marked our lives before we answered His call.

Once, while I was visiting Wheaton College in Illinois, a student came to me at the close of a chapel service. "All week long," he said, "you've told us how Christ wants to work through us—that He will do the work if we just allow Him to be Lord of our lives. My question is this: How can Jesus work through us without destroying our personality?"

In answering him, an illustration came to my mind. "When you prepare breakfast," I said, "you can plug an electric toaster and an electric mixer into the same outlet. The same electricity will power both appliances. Does that mean that they will both perform the same task?"

His face lit up with understanding. "I see what you mean," he said.

When God's power flows through two different people, He is able to work through them both. But no two people are alike. The way He energizes your life will produce different results from the way He energizes mine. Jesus is the one who lives in us and manifests Himself through us, but the result always reflects our individuality and personality.

Many books, video and cassette tape products, and seminar speakers will promise you unlimited power of some sort—the power to move you toward your goals, the power to make you a better salesman or executive, the power to make you rich and famous and sought-after. If you sign up for one of these courses or buy one of these books, you will be subjected to a standardized process designed to fit you into a mold. Everyone who buys the book, listens to the tapes, or attends the seminars will emerge thinking, talking, and acting much like everyone else who did the same. Unfortunately we do this to people in Christian circles as well. We subject people to our Christian programs in the way we'd feed meat to a sausage grinder. What comes out the other end of the sausage grinder? Identical little sausages!

But Jesus does not do that. He fills us with His power, and He acts through us, but we don't lose our individuality. Instead, we retain our individuality while gaining His.

The Comprehension and Insight of Jesus

Mark then records the second mark of Jesus' authority, His remarkable comprehension and insight.

> *They went to Capernaum, and when the Sabbath came, Jesus went into the synagogue and began to teach. The people were amazed at his teaching, because he taught them as one who had authority, not as the teachers of the law.*
>
> (MARK 1:21–22)

Notice the first word of that passage: "they." This refers to Peter, Andrew, James, and John, who accompanied Jesus into Capernaum.

In this passage, Mark is impressed by the comprehension of Jesus—the vast scope of His knowledge and insight into human life and the human condition. Mark was particularly impressed with the authority with which Jesus spoke. In fact, he notes that all who were present were astonished at His authority. Jesus did not teach like the scribes, who would say, "Now, Hillel says this, and Gamaliel adds that, while other authorities contend something different altogether."

Jesus did not cite any authority but Himself. Yet His words were so insightful, so true to experience, so sound and meaningful, that those who heard Him couldn't help but nod in agreement. To hear Him was to know that He spoke the truth. His words had the ring of truth; they were self-authenticating and corresponded to the inner conviction of each person who heard. No earthly authority has the right to judge the teaching of Jesus; instead, every earthly teaching must be judged and measured against what Jesus taught. He is the true authority.

During the Vietnam war era, when campuses across the United States were being torn by unrest and riots, I went to a Christian college to speak to a student gathering. I was surprised and dismayed to discover that even this Christian campus had not been spared from the worldly "question everything" attitude sweeping the land. I was invited to teach a class on current events, and we discussed various issues of the day: rampant immorality, capital punishment, civil rights, and the Vietnam war. I was dismayed to hear student after student cite the opinions of secular experts and authorities on these issues, yet no one was citing the answers given in God's Word. Finally I stopped the discussion and said, "You know, this is a Christian college. Yet no one in this class has made any reference at all to what God has to say about these matters. I submit to you that ultimately His viewpoint is the only viewpoint that counts. And it is in what He says that the truth lies."

Truth is what you find in the teachings of Jesus. We are not to assess the Word of God in light of modern psychology and philosophy. Rather, we are to correct our psychology and our philosophy by the truth that God has set forth in His Word. When we accept Jesus as our ultimate authority, we discover that the truths He first spoke some two thousand years ago demonstrate a depth of insight that secular doctors of the soul are only now beginning to grasp. As the American psychiatrist J. T. Fisher once observed,

> If you were to take the sum total of all authoritative articles ever written by the most qualified of psychologists and psychiatrists on the subject of mental hygiene— if you were to take the whole of the meat and none of the

parsley, and if you were to have these unadulterated bits of pure scientific knowledge concisely expressed by the most capable of living poets, you would have an awkward and incomplete summation of the Sermon on the Mount. For nearly two thousand years the Christian world has been holding in its hands the complete answer to its restless and fruitless yearnings. Here ... rests the blueprint for successful human life with optimum mental health and contentment.[1]

Now we begin to see why the people in the synagogue at Capernaum were astonished at the teaching of Jesus. As I read through the Scriptures and see the things Jesus said, I confess that I too am frequently amazed by the wisdom and psychological insight He displays. He is the authority on all things pertaining to life, relationships, meaning, peace, and happiness.

The Response to Jesus' Authority

The third mark of Jesus' authority is the remarkable response His teaching stirred that Sabbath morning.

> *Just then a man in their synagogue who was possessed by an evil spirit cried out, "What do you want with us, Jesus of Nazareth? Have you come to destroy us? I know who you are—the Holy One of God!"*
>
> *"Be quiet!" said Jesus sternly. "Come out of him!" The evil spirit shook the man violently and came out of him with a shriek.*
>
> *The people were all so amazed that they asked each other, "What is this? A new teaching—and with authority! He even gives orders to evil spirits and they obey him." News*

about him spread quickly over the whole region of Galilee.
(MARK 1:23–28)

Mark sums it up for us in the response of the people in the synagogue. They were astonished and said, "What is this? A new teaching—and with authority! He even gives orders to evil spirits and they obey him." The unclean spirit obeyed the command of Jesus. Our Lord's insight was so piercing and penetrating that it shone an unbearable light on the demon that lurked within the man. Tortured by the intensity of the truth that Jesus revealed, the demon angrily interrupted Him: "What do you want with us, Jesus of Nazareth? Have you come to destroy us? I know who you are—the Holy One of God!" And Jesus commanded the demon to be silent.

This account presents us with our Lord's first recorded encounter with the phenomenon that is popularly called demon possession. The Greek New Testament never uses the words "demon possession," although the New International Version does refer to a man who was "possessed by an evil spirit." "Demon possession" is a popular term that was coined aside from the Bible and may or may not be accurate from the perspective of Scripture. The word in Scripture is always "demonized." Whether it means possession or control or influence, this is the word that is used.

When *The Exorcist* (1973) was released, audiences streamed to the theaters to see it, and many people emerged from the darkened theaters screaming, crying, vomiting, or fainting. After watching the film, some people worried that they had become demon possessed. I never watched the film, but I have read several reviews. It is the story of a girl inhabited by a demon, an evil spirit. She is supposedly set free (exorcised) by two men who intercede on her behalf. But although the girl is freed (temporarily, perhaps) from the evil spirit, the story does not end in the triumph of good over evil. It is the demon who triumphs, for he destroys the two men in the process. *The Exorcist* is an evil and frightening film.

It is instructive to contrast the story of *The Exorcist*, a popular, secular notion of demon possession, with the biblical account of Jesus' encounter with a demon, as recorded by Mark. When Jesus confronts the evil spirit, the demon is driven out of the man. The word of Jesus is victorious from the start. There is no moral ambiguity, no partial victory. While the evil spirit is reluctant to go, as demonstrated by the way it convulses the man and cries out with a loud voice, the demon has no choice. Jesus speaks a command, and the evil spirit is overwhelmed by an infinitely superior power.

Throughout all the centuries since that day, the only name demons have ever feared is the name of Jesus. Jesus sets people free and delivers the oppressed. It is well to remember, when we face the forces of spiritual evil, no religious mumbo jumbo, no church ritual or chants or Latin words, no religious talismans or symbols or amulets have any power to set people free. It is Jesus alone whom demons fear. He has the authority to command unclean spirits.

So amazing was this event that, as Mark records, "news about him spread quickly over the whole region of Galilee." When Mark says "quickly," he does not mean in a few days or weeks; he means in a few hours. This was such a remarkable situation that within hours the word spread like wildfire all through the region. By evening, people by the scores were bringing the sick and demonized into the city to be healed by Jesus, as we will soon see. When the people heard that here was one who commanded the spirits of darkness and they obeyed, they had to see for themselves.

The Compassion of Jesus

The next event in this day in the life of Jesus is the account of a simple event in the home of Simon and Andrew.

> *As soon as they left the synagogue, they went with James and John to the home of Simon and Andrew. Simon's mother-in-law was in bed with a fever, and they told Jesus about her. So he went to her, took her hand and helped her up. The fever left her and she began to wait on them.* (MARK 1:29–31)

It is early afternoon, and Mark's emphasis is on the compassion that moved Jesus. Simon and Andrew had invited Jesus, James, and John home with them, only to find that Simon's mother-in-law was sick. So they mentioned the woman to Jesus and explained that she was unwell. From the English phrase "they told Jesus about her," you might get the idea that they also asked Jesus to heal her. But the Greek makes it clear that they mentioned to Jesus that the lady of the house was not feeling well and would not be able to offer any hospitality. Simon and Andrew had seen Jesus command an evil spirit out of a man, but they had never seen Him heal anyone. It almost certainly didn't occur to them that He could. Healing the woman was Jesus' idea, not theirs.

When Jesus heard about the woman's illness, He took the initiative, approached her, and laid His hand on her. Immediately the fever left her. Out of a grateful heart, this restored woman ministered to the needs of Jesus that afternoon.

It wasn't necessary that Jesus raise this woman up. She was not particularly sick. The fever doubtless would have run its course, and she would have recovered in a few days. But this incident speaks of the compassion of Jesus. Minor though her suffering might have been, Jesus responded to this woman's plight and restored her to joyful service. Mark records this event because he wants us to know that Jesus is compassionate and ministers with tenderness and love.

The Gathering Crowds

Now we come to the evening of the day, the culmination of all the events that have occurred in the morning, noon, and afternoon. The word of Jesus' amazing works has spread throughout the region, and this, as Mark records, is the result:

> *That evening after sunset the people brought to Jesus all the sick and demon-possessed. The whole town gathered at the door, and Jesus healed many who had various diseases. He also drove out many demons, but he would not let the demons speak because they knew who he was.*
>
> (MARK 1:32–34)

At sundown the Sabbath ended, and the people from all around began to bring the sick and demonized for Jesus to heal. Mark tells us the "whole town gathered at the door." If you visit Capernaum today, you will find only a small town, perhaps a half-dozen houses. The ruins of a synagogue are there. Some scholars believe it was the synagogue where Jesus taught. Although most scholars and archaeologists date the ruined synagogue from the second century, it was probably built on the site of the synagogue described in Mark's account. In Jesus' time, Capernaum was a flourishing lakeshore town, one of the largest in the region. It is where Jesus made His home.

The people brought their sick and demonized to be healed. What a busy, full evening Jesus spent there in Capernaum! Mark records for us the amazing control Jesus exercised over the demons that were brought before Him. He would not permit them to speak, and they obeyed because they knew Him. This is significant in that it shows that Jesus, far from wanting to be known as a wonder worker, wanted to deemphasize the spectacular, to keep it under control, to play down deliverance from demons and physical healing. On a number of occasions, Jesus told those He healed, "Go, and tell no one." Yet they invariably disobeyed Him, and in time He could no longer minister in the city because of the enormous crowds that followed Him. Jesus did not seek out the crowds, but He could not keep the crowds from seeking Him.

Contrast Jesus with the so-called healers of our day. They are masters of advertising, electronic media, and showmanship. Unlike Jesus, they want big crowds—the bigger the better. When we look at the physical healings that Jesus performed, and later, the healings performed by His apostles, we always see that the spectacular aspect is played down, not trumpeted or advertised. There is no record in Scripture of people giving public testimonials in order to increase the crowds, or dramatic displays of crutches lined up to impress the masses. The exploitation of healings for donations or human ego gratification is unbiblical and unlike Christ.

Does God still heal today as He did in Jesus' day? Of course God heals, and we should thank God for physical healings. But we must keep this issue in perspective. Physical healings are only temporary blessings at best. What Jesus continually emphasizes is the healing of the soul and spirit of people—the healing of sin, bitterness, faultfinding, hostility, lust, gossip, anger, worry, and anxiety. This is what God wants to deliver us from, because spiritual deliverance is eternal deliverance, not merely a temporary blessing. That is why Jesus turns His back on popular acclaim.

The Interrupted Prayer of Jesus

It has been a long and busy day in the life of Jesus, but it is not over yet. Mark details for us one final event of that day.

> *Very early in the morning, while it was still dark, Jesus got up, left the house and went off to a solitary place, where he prayed. Simon and his companions went to look for him, and when they found him, they exclaimed: "Everyone is looking for you!"*
>
> *Jesus replied, "Let us go somewhere else—to the nearby villages—so I can preach there also. That is why I have come." So he traveled throughout Galilee, preaching in their synagogues and driving out demons.* (MARK 1:35–39)

After this full day, Mark records that early in the morning, before it was daylight, Jesus went out alone, climbed the mountainside, and prayed. But even there He was not safe from intrusion. His disciples interrupted His communion with the Father to tell Him the crowds were already seeking Him. Jesus reveals the heart and substance of His prayer in what He says in reply: "Let us go somewhere else—to the nearby villages—so I can preach there also. That is why I have come." He prayed for open doors and open hearts in the cities to which He would go next.

Why did Jesus take time alone with the Father while He faced so much pressure from the crowds and a busy schedule? He wanted to make clear to us that His authority came not from Him but from the Father. Again and again throughout the four gospels,

Jesus makes this point: He acts only on authority given Him by the Father.

We should never water down the deity of Christ, for He is fully God as well as fully man. But neither should we compromise the amazing truth, which He stressed again and again, that He lived a life derived entirely from God the Father. In John 5:19, He said, "I tell you the truth, the Son can do nothing by himself; he can do only what he sees his Father doing, because whatever the Father does the Son also does." Again He says, "Don't you believe that I am in the Father, and that the Father is in me? The words I say to you are not just my own. Rather, it is the Father, living in me, who is doing his work" (John 14:10). How can we ignore what He is saying to us? Yes, He is the Son of God, but the power He manifests is the power that flows through Him from God the Father.

Why is this such an important point? Because Jesus wants us to understand that we are to operate on the same basis that He did. Whatever we face in life must be faced in total reliance on God. This is the secret of the Christian life. All power to live the Christian life comes not from us but from Him. Power is given to those who follow, those who obey. The Father is at work in the Son; the Son is at work in us. As we learn this, God's power is able to flow through us to meet the demands of our lives and the needs of the people around us.

This is why Jesus was up on the hillside praying. He wanted to build such an intensity of relationship with the Father that there would be no hindrance to the flow of the Spirit of God through Him as He went out to minister. What a difference it makes when we begin to understand this principle and when we derive our lives from God instead of operating from our easily depleted strength.

Once, after I had been teaching on this principle at a Christian college for a week, a student came to me and said, "I went back to my dorm last night with that message going through my mind: 'Everything coming from God; nothing coming from me.' I tried to concentrate on my studies, but my mind kept going out to my father, who was not a Christian. Finally I phoned him and said, 'Dad, there's a Billy Graham film playing in town. Why don't we go see it?' He said, 'Thanks, son, but I'm really too tired to go out tonight.' But I kept urging him, and finally he said, 'Okay, son, we haven't done anything together in a while. Let's go.' So we went—and my dad received the Lord as his Savior. I can't tell you how happy I am that I let God work through me that night!"

This is the truth we need to grasp. We strategize and organize and make our human plans. When we pray, it is not so much to seek God's power as to inform Him of our intentions and ask His blessing on our efforts. No wonder we fail! We leave no room for God to operate.

But Jesus knew the secret of effective living, and He modeled it for us. He showed that God will work in a unique, wonderful, and powerful way if only we let Him. We can achieve the unimaginable, if only we will become willing instruments in the hands of our awesome Creator.

That is the secret that impressed Mark: the secret of the authority of the servant. The one who serves is the one who rules. That is the great truth God seeks to teach us. If we will live as Jesus lived, drawing on the power of God as Jesus did, then God will work in us and through us.

On January 21, 1930, King George V of England was about to address the opening session of an international arms control conference in London. It was an event of intense interest around the world. The First World War had ended less than a decade and a half earlier, and the people of the world were anxious to prevent another world war. King George's speech was about to be carried around the globe by a relatively new technology called radio, but America almost didn't get to hear it.

Just minutes before the king of England stepped up to the microphones, a technician in the control room of the Columbia Broadcasting System tripped over a cable and severed the connection. The CBS control chief, a man named Harold Vidian, didn't even stop to think about what he was doing. He reached out, grasped the ends of the severed cable with his bare hands, and restored the circuit with his body.

Instantly Vidian was jolted by several hundred volts of electricity. He managed to hang on as King George's message was broadcast across the North American continent. Vidian survived—and the king's voice was heard.

That is an electrifying image of what our lives are to be like. We are the channels, the conductors of God's power. When we allow His power to course through us, then the voice of the King will be heard throughout the world.

The Healer of Hurts

➤ **Mark 1:40–2:12**

In his autobiography, *Timebends,* playwright Arthur Miller talks about his tumultuous marriage to screen idol Marilyn Monroe. In contrast to her "dumb blonde" screen image, Miller found her to be a bright and thoughtful woman who was often in the grip of deep depression and despair. Although Marilyn had been reared in a conservative Christian home and Miller was reared Jewish, neither believed in God anymore.

Marilyn regularly went to a well-known psychoanalyst who prescribed large amounts of barbiturates for her. Perhaps because of the drugs, she was becoming increasingly paranoid, fearing that someone was trying to kill her. One night, after the doctor had given Marilyn a tranquilizer to help her sleep, Miller stood over her bed, watching her. It seemed to him that the only peaceful moments she ever knew were when she slept. He reflected,

> I found myself straining to imagine miracles. What if she were to wake and I were able to say: "God loves you, darling." And what if she were able to believe it? How I wish I still had my religion and she, hers.

How tragic! For the truth is that we don't have to strain to imagine miracles. The miracle worker has come. God does love us. And He brings hope and healing to broken lives and wounded hearts.

Jesus is the Healer of hurts.

Jesus' Knowledge of Our Humanity

We come at this point to a natural division in Mark's gospel, one of several such divisions. The first section is Mark 1:1–39. Each division of Mark's gospel ends with a summary statement, such as this one in Mark 1:39: "So he [Jesus] traveled throughout Galilee, preaching in their synagogues and driving out demons." The theme of the first division of Mark is the authority of the Servant—the authority Jesus exercised as He commanded the disciples to follow Him, and they followed; as He commanded the evil spirits to be silent and depart, and they obeyed; as He commanded illnesses to vanish and fevers to subside, and they did.

The next natural division is Mark 1:40–3:6. The theme of this second division is Jesus' knowledge of our humanity. In this section, we repeatedly see His perceptive understanding of who we are and why we act the way we do. The apostle John expresses this same facet of Jesus' character in his gospel:

> *Now while he was in Jerusalem at the Passover Feast, many people saw the miraculous signs he was doing and believed in his name. But Jesus would not entrust himself to them, for he knew all men. He did not need man's testimony about man, for he knew what was in a man.* (JOHN 2:23–25)

That significant statement means that Jesus knew every individual who came to Him. That is why He could say to Nathanael,

"I saw you while you were still under the fig tree before Philip called you" (John 1:48). That is why He could tell Nicodemus that he needed to be born again (John 3:3) and why He could say to the woman at the well, "The fact is, you have had five husbands, and the man you now have is not your husband" (John 4:18). He had a deep knowledge of people He had never met. Why? Because He knew what was in a person. He understood our humanity, how God made us, and who we are. That is the theme Mark develops in the second division of his gospel.

This division opens with two incidents in the life of Jesus: the healing of a leper and the healing of a paralytic. These incidents are linked by the way they reveal a deep truth about humanity and the way they reveal Jesus' perfect knowledge of our human nature. The story of the healing of the leper is found in Mark 1:40–42. Comparing this passage with the parallel passage in Matthew, we find that Matthew places the healing of the leper immediately after the Sermon on the Mount. As Jesus was coming down the mountain, this leper met Him. Mark describes the incident in this way:

> *A man with leprosy came to him and begged him on his knees, "If you are willing, you can make me clean."*
>
> *Filled with compassion, Jesus reached out his hand and touched the man. "I am willing," he said. "Be clean!" Immediately the leprosy left him and he was cured.*
>
> (MARK 1:40–42)

In this scene, Jesus heals a man who is infected with leprosy, a once common plague now known as Hansen's disease. Mark highlights two impressive things about this miracle: the appeal of this leper to the will of Jesus, which is unique among the recorded miracles of Jesus; and the compassionate response with which Jesus answers the leper's appeal. It is significant and instructive that the leper says to Jesus, "If you are willing, you can make me clean."

"If You Are Willing, Lord"

A young man once came to me with the issue of healing on his mind. He had been influenced by the teaching of the name-it-and-claim-it movement that had swept many churches. This movement teaches that God always heals if we ask in faith, that it is wrong (and even a sin) to be sick, and that we never have to ask God whether or not it is His will to heal us. The result of this teaching is that if a person becomes sick and is not healed, then he or she is accused of lacking faith or having sin in his or her life. The pain of accusation then is added to the person's physical suffering.

This young man told me, "When we pray, 'If it be your will, please heal me,' we are demonstrating a lack of faith. It's always God's will to heal us! The phrase 'if it be your will' is just a cop-out, a way of covering up for our lack of faith. Then, if we aren't healed, we can shrug and say, 'I guess it wasn't God's will.' The fact is, we lacked the faith to claim God's healing for our lives." The young man was adamant.

I reminded the young man of the story of this leper and of the first words out of his mouth when he came to Jesus: "If you are willing, you can make me clean." I said, "You know, Jesus did not rebuke the leper for a lack of faith. He didn't tell the leper, 'That's not the way to ask.' In fact, I challenge you to show me where in the Scriptures you find a statement that we should claim a healing from God."

The young man couldn't name any Scripture passage in support of this teaching. There is no biblical defense for the idea that our will should take precedence over the will of God. Our prayers should always be like that of the leper: "if you are willing, Lord."

In this story, we see the leper's keen awareness of a divine purpose for even something as terrible as leprosy. It may be difficult for us to accept, but the Scriptures teach that God sometimes allows us, in His perfect will, to become sick. It is not that God is mean or cruel. But there are times when God allows His children, whom He loves, to pass through times of physical affliction. You see numerous examples of this in the Scriptures.

Paul, for example, came before the Lord and asked three times for the removal of a physical "thorn in [the] flesh" (see 2 Corinthians 12:7). That thorn in the flesh was a physical ailment of some sort. Although we are not told specifically what Paul suffered from, we know it was serious and debilitating, because Paul earnestly asked God to heal him of it. Finally the answer came from God: "My grace is sufficient for you, for my power is made perfect in weakness." So Paul concluded, "Therefore I will boast all the more gladly about my weaknesses, so that Christ's power may rest on me" (2 Corinthians 12:9). Paul understood that God wanted him to accept his condition, endure it by the grace of God, and press on in ministry. Paul accepted the fact that God had a purpose for his pain.

The leper also sensed a purpose in his pain. When he said, "If you are willing, you can make me clean," he didn't mean, "If you're in a good mood right now." Instead, he meant, "If my request is not out of line with God's purpose, then you can make me clean." Jesus' response is moving. "Filled with compassion," writes Mark, "Jesus reached out his hand and touched the man. 'I am willing,' he said. 'Be clean!' Immediately the leprosy left him and he was cured." That statement, "I am willing," is like a green light from God, a signal that the time has come for healing to occur. God is about to use this man's leprosy to further His eternal plan.

Mark shows us the motive that moved Jesus: compassion. Moreover, Mark records that Jesus "reached out his hand and touched the man." It is important to understand what it means when Mark says that Jesus touched the leper. Few things in this world are more horrific or repulsive than a body that is infected with leprosy. This man was not in the first stages of leprosy; his condition was advanced. We know this because Luke's parallel account of this incident states that the man "was covered with leprosy" (Luke 5:12). William Barclay gives us a description of a victim of this terrible disease:

> The whole appearance of the face is changed, till the man loses his human appearance and looks, as the ancients said, "like a lion or a satyr." The nodules grow larger and larger. They ulcerate. From them comes a foul discharge. The eyebrows fall out, the eyes become staring. The voice becomes hoarse, and the breath wheezes because of the ulceration of the vocal chords. The hands and the feet always ulcerate. Slowly the sufferer becomes a mass of ulcerated growths. The average course of the disease is nine years, and it ends in mental decay, coma, and ultimately death. The sufferer becomes utterly repulsive—both to himself and to others.[1]

One of the worst aspects of leprosy is the sense of worthlessness and disgust generated by this disease. The sufferer is a thing of horror to everyone around. Lepers are feared and shunned. They are unclean. But this man comes to Jesus, breaking the Levitical law against lepers' association with other people. He dares to kneel before Jesus and ask to be healed. So Jesus reaches out and lovingly touches the man, an action that also violates Levitical law. But when Jesus touches him, the leprosy vanishes. The man's flesh is healthy, whole, and clean. This beautiful incident illustrates the power and compassion of Jesus.

From Plan A to Plan B

Even though the leper begins with an attitude of faith and humility in his approach to Jesus, he is about to disobey Jesus, forcing the Lord to move from plan A to plan B. Mark's account continues:

> *Jesus sent him away at once with a strong warning: "See that you don't tell this to anyone. But go, show yourself to the priest and offer the sacrifices that Moses commanded for your cleansing, as a testimony to them."* (MARK 1:43–44)

Note that last phrase: "as a testimony to them." As a testimony to whom? Some versions add the words "to the people," but that is not what the Greek says. Jesus is telling the healed leper to present himself as a testimony to the priests. Here we see what Jesus intended to accomplish by healing this man. He intended to show the power of God to the priests at the temple, to the religious leaders of Israel. It was to be a sign of the Messiah.

Imagine the consternation of the religious leaders as this man, who was known to have advanced leprosy, came to them, clean and whole. They would go to their libraries, mumble over their books, and ask each other, "What do we do? There's never been anything like this since the days of Elisha!" Until then, the last recorded instance of a healing from leprosy was in 2 Kings 5. And even then it wasn't an Israelite but a Gentile who was healed (Naaman, commander of the Syrian armies). Jesus knew that the priests would be dumbfounded over the meaning of this miracle.

This was part of the Lord's plan: to manifest a sign of the Messiah. Everyone in Israel, and especially the priests, knew that leprosy was a symbol of the evil and sin of humankind. At times God had used leprosy as a form of judgment against sin. It demonstrated in visible form what the invisible infection of sin is like in God's sight. Isaiah had predicted that when Messiah would come, He would accomplish physical miracles of healing. Here, then, was one of the signs of the Messiah, which Jesus intended that the priests should see, as a testimony of who He was.

But this testimony was lost by the disobedience of the leper. Mark records what the leper did next.

> *Instead he went out and began to talk freely, spreading the news. As a result, Jesus could no longer enter a town openly but stayed outside in lonely places. Yet the people still came to him from everywhere.* (MARK 1:45)

The leper was a blabbermouth! He could not keep quiet, even though Jesus had told him that he should tell no one but the priests. The healed leper was to go to the official representatives of the nation as a sign and a witness to them that the Messiah had come. Instead, the man succumbed to the desire to tell everyone what had happened.

It is understandable that he would feel this way. Who wouldn't? And I don't believe Jesus intended the man to remain silent forever, only that he should not spread the news until he had given his testimony to the priests. But the man couldn't contain himself, and this account shows that obedience is better than praise.

I don't say this to point a finger of blame at this man, for he didn't do anything that you and I don't do on a regular basis. Again and again, we set aside the Scriptures and disobey what God has said, thinking we know what is best in this or that situation. We excuse our disobedience on the grounds that we have the best of intentions. But we are fooling ourselves. No one ever has a good excuse to disobey God.

Perhaps Jesus' ministry in Jerusalem would have been much more effective if the healed leper had obeyed. By disregarding Jesus' word, the man forced Jesus to go to plan B. He could not go into the cities, as He had originally planned, but instead had to stay in the countryside. This healed leper, full of joy and gratitude but disobedient to the word of Jesus, is a testimony to you and me of the need to take the Lord at His word and do what He says, no more, no less. When we think we have a better plan, we only get in the way of God's plan.

The Faith of Five Men

In the opening verse of Mark 2, Mark moves on to another healing, that of the paralytic. This story divides into two parts, the first part centering on the faith of five men.

A few days later, when Jesus again entered Capernaum, the people heard that he had come home. So many gathered that there was no room left, not even outside the door, and he preached the word to them. Some men came, bringing to him a paralytic, carried by four of them. Since they could not get him to Jesus because of the crowd, they made an opening in the roof above Jesus and, after digging through it, lowered the mat the paralyzed man was lying on. When Jesus saw

their faith, he said to the paralytic, "Son, your sins are for-
*given." (*MARK *2:1–5)*

The obvious thing Mark underscores is the faith and determination of these five men. This was not a healing service they had broken into. Jesus was preaching inside a house. In context, it seems likely that He was avoiding the streets because He could hardly go anywhere without being besieged with people needing to be healed or released from demon possession. But His first priority was to preach the Word of the kingdom.

So Jesus had isolated Himself in a house, and the room was jammed with people. Even the doorway was blocked. But five men—a paralyzed man and the four friends who brought him—were determined to reach Jesus. Our Lord uses this incident to suggest to us that God is always open to the needs of people, regardless of whether those needs are physical, spiritual, or emotional. If a person's desire is strong enough, He will respond, whatever the agenda might have been. I love those times of serendipity and surprise when the Spirit of God ignores the agenda. Healing the paralyzed man was not on Jesus' program that day, but it soon became the focus of His attention.

This incident is a memorable commentary on a statement of Jesus recorded in another gospel. In Matthew 11:12, Jesus says, "From the days of John the Baptist until now, the kingdom of heaven has been forcefully advancing, and forceful men lay hold of it." Many people have wondered what He meant by that. But Jesus is telling us, "Look, I'm ready to give to those who want it enough to come and lay hold of it." If you want the kingdom of heaven in your life, God will give it. So these men came, forcefully, intrusively, ready to take what they knew God was offering at that moment. They came to lay hold of the kingdom of heaven and the promise of God.

Here we see what faith is all about. There are three remarkable and beautiful aspects of it.

First, these men dared to do the difficult. That is where faith always manifests itself. It was not easy to bring this man to the Lord. They had to carry him, who knows how far, through the streets of the city. When they arrived, they found the doorway blocked. Did that stop them? No! The four friends carried the paralyzed man up an outside stairway to the roof. It is not easy to carry a full-grown man up a flight of stairs, yet these four determined men managed the task. They dared to do the difficult. This is a powerful illustration of what we should dare in order to bring people to Christ.

Second, these men dared to do the unorthodox. To say the least, it is frowned on to break up somebody's roof. But these men were not afraid to be unorthodox. They were not afraid to interrupt the meeting or break a few clay tiles to bring their friend to Jesus. They did what they had to do to get the job done. They were outside-the-box thinkers. They were creative. And it is instructive to notice that Jesus never rebukes them.

Most Christians today, unfortunately, live by the motto "Come weal or come woe, our status is quo." We are afraid to rock the boat, afraid to raise eyebrows, afraid to be criticized, afraid to be thought unorthodox. I applaud these men who did whatever they had to do in order to reach Jesus, not caring what anyone thought. I pray that you and I would be as daring and unconventional in our efforts to bring people to Christ.

Third, they dared to do the costly. Somebody had to pay for that roof. Imagine the expression on the face of the homeowner as chunks of tile began raining from his ceiling and a patch of blue sky opened overhead. He probably wondered if his home-owner's policy covered such an eventuality. Very likely he presented a bill to the four friends of the paralyzed man, and perhaps they gladly split the bill four ways. What was the cost of a few tiles compared with the welfare of their friend? They dared to do the costly. That is faith! That is a challenge to us to do whatever it takes to bring people to Christ.

The Protest of the Scribes

Mark begins by emphasizing the extraordinary faith and perseverance of these five men. Then he moves to the second part of the story, which gathers around the protest of the scribes. Here we find the heart of the story. As we move to this part of the story, keep in mind the words of Jesus to the paralyzed man at the end of Mark 2:5: "Son, your sins are forgiven." Now read the response of the scribes:

> Some teachers of the law were sitting there, thinking to themselves, "Why does this fellow talk like that? He's blaspheming! Who can forgive sins but God alone?"
>
> Immediately Jesus knew in his spirit that this was what they were thinking in their hearts, and he said to them, "Why are you thinking these things? Which is easier: to say to the paralytic, 'Your sins are forgiven,' or to say, 'Get up, take your mat and walk'? But that you may know that the Son of Man has authority on earth to forgive sins . . . . " He said to the paralytic, "I tell you, get up, take your mat and go home." He got up, took his mat and walked out in full view of them all. This amazed everyone and they praised God, saying, "We have never seen anything like this!" (MARK 2:6–12)

It is evident from Jesus' words that this paralysis was caused by some moral difficulty. Our Lord's insight was accurate and keen. He understood instantly what was wrong with this man. Notice that He did not begin at the physical but at the spiritual: "Son, your sins are forgiven." In fact, Matthew tells us He said, "Take heart, son; your sins are forgiven" (Matthew 9:2). This indicates that the paralysis was what doctors sometimes call emotionally induced or psychosomatic illness.

Doctors have said that 50 percent of all the illnesses they treat have an emotional basis. This is not to say that the person isn't truly sick; he or she probably is. But our emotions often help to bring on such illnesses as digestive disorders, heart problems, respiratory problems, high blood pressure, and more. The patient is genuinely sick, but the sickness is emotionally induced. The emotional issues that can produce physical illnesses include bitterness, resentment, unforgiveness, anger, guilt, worry, and so forth. It has been well said that ulcers are caused not by what you eat but by what is eating you.

Knowing all of this, Jesus went to the heart of the problem. He touched the man and said, "Son, your sins are forgiven." If He had healed the paralysis without forgiving the sin, the paralysis would have returned, sooner or later. This accounts for many of the so-called miracles of healing in the healing services we hear and read about today. These often involve emotionally induced physical problems. The momentary atmosphere of excitement and faith generated by such a meeting can effect a temporary healing, but medical investigators have proven again and again that these illnesses generally return in a few days or weeks, after the faith healer has moved on to the next town. But our Lord went to the heart of the matter and began with forgiveness. He wanted this man to be healed indeed.

This was a problem for the scribes sitting nearby. Notice how Mark describes their consternation: they were "thinking to themselves." They did not speak aloud, not even to talk among themselves. Even so, Jesus read their thoughts. You can imagine the startled looks on their faces when our Lord turned to them and said, "Why are you fellows thinking that way? I know what you're thinking."

Some readers would interpret Jesus' insight into their thinking as evidence of His omniscience (ability to know all) as God. I do not think so. There were many things that Jesus told us flatly that He didn't know, such as the hour of His second coming. I am convinced that His keen insight into our humanity was not a manifestation of divine omniscience. Rather, it was the manifestation of the spiritual gift of discernment in its fullest degree. Peter displayed the same gift when Ananias and Sapphira lied about a donation they made to the church (see Acts 5:1–11). He knew all about their fraud, even though no one had told him. Similarly, when Paul was confronted on the island of Cyprus by a sorcerer named Bar-Jesus, the apostle saw through him and knew the attitude of his heart (see Acts 13:6–12).

Our Lord knew what was going on in the minds of these scribes. So He proposed a test: "Which is easier: to say to the paralytic, 'Your sins are forgiven,' or to say, 'Get up, take your mat and walk'?" Any charlatan or religious fake can say, "Your sins are forgiven," and no one could prove whether it happened or not. But Jesus did better than that. He was saying, "You question my ability to forgive sins. Fine. I'm going to demonstrate to you that I not only have the power to forgive sins but the power to heal as well. You can verify whether or not this man is truly healed. And if he is truly healed, then his sins are truly forgiven as well."

Then, turning to the paralyzed man, Jesus said, "Get up, take your mat and go home." The man obeyed. He was instantly healed. Before their eyes, he walked out of their midst. All the people, except the scribes, rejoiced and gave glory to God, saying, "We've never seen anything like this before!"

What amazed them? I am convinced it was not merely the healing. I believe they were even more amazed by Jesus' understanding of the problems of human nature. He understood so clearly that physical and emotional problems are often caused by spiritual disease and maladjustment. He understood that true healing and deliverance lie not in merely curing an illness but in restoring a right relationship between a person and God. This is what amazed them.

Do you struggle with bitterness and unforgiveness? With guilt? With fear, worry, or anxiety? Do you struggle with a broken family relationship or friendship? Our Lord offers healing to you on the same terms as He offered it to the paralyzed man. Your healing begins with your relationship to God. Only the person who has heard Jesus say, "Your sins are forgiven," is free to experience true healing in all the other areas of his or her life.

Our Lord understood the need of the paralyzed man, and He instantly went to the heart of that need. He told the man, "Son, the one thing you need more than anything else is to have your sins forgiven. So take heart, be of good cheer, your sins are forgiven." After that, it was the easiest thing imaginable to cure the paralysis of the man's life.

The Healer of hurts has come, and the first hurt He wants to heal is the hurt of sin and guilt. Forgiveness is the first miracle of healing He wants to do in your life and mine. Every other work of healing in our lives flows from the miracle of His forgiving love.

five

The Scandal Maker

➤ **Mark 2:13–3:6**

During the 1700s, two English evangelists stepped out of their stone-and-stained-glass cloisters and took the Christian gospel into the countryside, into the coal mines and prisons and infirmaries. Their names: George Whitefield and John Wesley. As they went preaching in places where the gospel had never been before, they encountered scorn and ridicule, not so much from the unchurched and the unwashed as from their brethren, from the religious leaders, the high and holy churchmen of their time. Whitefield and Wesley scandalized the leaders of the church.

The gospel, sniffed the religious elite, is not for the streets and fields, the hospital deathbeds and mineshafts. No, the gospel must be preserved and enshrined in stone cathedrals. If people want to hear the gospel, let them come to church, sit in pews, and hear it preached from pulpits in the proper way. But do not go out where the people live and work, for the gospel may get sullied out there among the riffraff.

But Whitefield and Wesley ignored the sanctimonious and scandalized churchmen. They were a pair of scandal makers, following in the footsteps of the great scandal maker, Jesus Christ.

Today a battle still rages between the scandalized and the scandal makers. In many churches, the old gospel is going out in new ways. Christians are discovering and using exciting new media for communicating the gospel. The old story is being told in new settings: in crisis pregnancy centers and urban youth clubs and homeless shelters and abused women's shelters. Churches are sprouting up that no longer look and sound like the churches of old. The music is new, fresh, and exciting, played on guitars and drums instead of massive pipe organs. The Word is not only preached but also acted out, danced, sung, and projected on video screens.

To some people, this is scandalous. If pipe organs and stained glass were good enough for the eighteenth century, they are good enough for the twenty-first. Why should we change the way we communicate the gospel? God doesn't change; why should we? Why should we take the gospel to the malls and the city parks and the kids at the beach? If anyone wants to hear the good news, they know where to find it. The church isn't going anywhere. Let them scrub themselves up, put on their Sunday best, and come to our place of worship. Let *them* change, not us. If they will come to our church and adopt our ways, then we will share the gospel with them.

The scandalized religious leaders are still with us, but so are the Christian scandal makers, following in the footsteps of the great scandal maker, Jesus Christ.

Our Lord never hesitated to flout petty human regulations and to outrage the arrogant sensibilities of the powerful. In the next portion of Mark's gospel, we will see Him knowingly and deliberately offend people. We will see Him became too hot to handle, so that the establishment finally conspires to rid itself of Him. Although Jesus was never violent, although He was not a militant or a radical revolutionary, as some people have tried to paint him, He definitely challenged the status quo.

So let's delve deeper into Mark's gospel. Let's meet Jesus the scandal maker.

The Calling of Matthew the Tax Collector

We come to the final portion of the second division of Mark's gospel. We have already seen Jesus' penetrating knowledge of human nature, the clarity of that knowledge was reflected in the healings of the leper and the paralyzed man. Now Mark brings together four incidents that reveal the confrontational side of Jesus' nature. He refuses to be boxed in by purely human regulations, so He provokes a controversy to make evident the true nature of our freedom in Him. The stage is set by Jesus' calling of Matthew, a tax collector, to be one of His disciples.

> *Once again Jesus went out beside the lake. A large crowd came to him, and he began to teach them. As he walked along, he saw Levi son of Alphaeus sitting at the tax collector's booth. "Follow me," Jesus told him, and Levi got up and followed him.* (MARK 2:13–14)

Levi evidently was Matthew's given name. It is likely that Jesus is the one who changed his name to Matthew, because He renamed several disciples. He said to Simon the son of Jonas, "You shall be called Peter" (the Rock), and He nicknamed James and John, sons of Zebedee, "the Sons of Thunder." It is likely, although Scripture does not say so, that Jesus changed Levi's name to Matthew, which means "gift of God." Perhaps that is how Jesus thought of him.

Levi lived and worked in Capernaum, where Jesus had made His home. Levi was a tax collector and must have known of Jesus and heard Him speak, even before this call. It is remarkable that Jesus would call a man like this, for tax collectors were even more disliked in those days than IRS agents are today. For the most part, they were government-licensed extortionists and racketeers, making their living by taxing the people beyond what the law demanded. They turned in a percentage to the government and kept the rest. They had sold out to the Roman oppressors and were traitors to their people.

Jesus saw something in Levi that no one else saw. The Lord knew Levi's heart. He knew something in this tax collector made him discontented with his life. He saw the hunger in Levi's heart. So He called Levi and said, "Follow me." Did Jesus know that by accepting such a hated man as His disciple He would open Himself up to criticism and opposition? Did He realize what a scandal it would create?

Yes, He knew.

An Outreach to Outcasts

The next scene Mark records probably occurred on the following day. Mark writes:

> While Jesus was having dinner at Levi's house, many tax collectors and "sinners" were eating with him and his disciples, for there were many who followed him. When the teachers of the law who were Pharisees saw him eating with the "sinners" and tax collectors, they asked his disciples: "Why does he eat with tax collectors and 'sinners'?"
>
> On hearing this, Jesus said to them, "It is not the healthy who need a doctor, but the sick. I have not come to call the righteous, but sinners." (MARK 2:15–17)

This evidently was a farewell dinner Matthew gave for his friends, his tax-collecting buddies. He was saying farewell to his work and friends and leaving to follow Jesus from place to place. It was also an opportunity to introduce his friends to his new-found Lord. This feast was therefore a normal, natural occasion of festivity and joy.

What a collection of lowlifes must have been there that day! All the tax collectors of the city, all the sinners, all the despised social outcasts were sitting there. As the scribes and the Pharisees passed by, they saw what probably looked like the equivalent of a modern beer party, with open bottles of Coors, playing cards and poker chips, loud laughter and bawdy talk. And there, in the midst of it all, sat Jesus of Nazareth! And these scribes, these dignified religious leaders, were outraged, incensed, scandalized.

The closer they looked, the more scandalized they became. Jesus wasn't lecturing the lowlifes. He wasn't berating and condemning them. He was eating and drinking with them. He acted as if He were their friend. The scribes lost their composure. They called the disciples aside and demanded, "Why does Jesus associate with those dregs and social outcasts? Doesn't He know who those people are?"

Jesus hears their question and gives them a surprising, revealing answer. In fact, He agrees with them. He says, "You're absolutely right! These are sick, hurting, troubled men. Their way of life has damaged them deeply. They don't see life rightly. They are sick men. But where should a doctor be but among the sick?" That is His argument. Jesus came to heal, so it only makes sense that He went among those who needed healing.

In that marvelous way Jesus has of putting things, He directs the Pharisees' attention back on themselves. He says, "I have not come to call the righteous, but sinners." Of course, Jesus knows that no one is righteous and that all are sinners. But He also knows that the Pharisees think themselves righteous, even though they are much more wretched and lost in sin than these social outcasts. At least the outcasts knew they needed a Savior. The smug, self-righteous Pharisees refused to admit they were sick.

So the message of Jesus to the Pharisees was, "To those who think they're righteous, I have nothing to say. But these outcasts that you look down on know they're sick, and they are ready and open to receiving my help. That is why I have come to them. That is why I am a friend to them." Our Lord made two truths emphatic by this reply.

First, people who cannot admit their need of God will receive no help from God. God has nothing to say to them. That is why many people are unable to turn to God until the bottom drops out of their lives. Some will turn to God only when their drinking or drug use destroys their health or their family; or when they are in the hospital with a life-threatening injury or illness; or when they have suffered a financial collapse or the loss of their reputation. As long as people are self-sufficient, as long as everything is going smoothly in their lives, they have no need of God. So God, in His infinite love and mercy, will sometimes allow trouble to enter our lives, not to destroy us but to turn our hearts toward Him.

I once knew a prominent, successful attorney. He had money, he was riding high, he had no need of God. Then a series of business reversals brought him to the brink of bankruptcy. His wife grew tired of the financial problems and announced she was leaving him. This attorney became depressed and suicidal. He realized that he could no longer handle life, and at the moment of that realization, he became open to the gospel.

God will do whatever He must to shatter the illusion that we can handle life by ourselves. He does this not to hurt us but to heal us. Just as a surgeon must sometimes take a scalpel and inflict pain in order to remove the thing that is destroying our health, the Great Physician must sometimes inflict a surgical kind of pain on us in order that we can be healed.

This doesn't mean that trials come only to those who live outside of God's will. Trials come into every life, including the lives of those who trust and obey Him. But if we will submit ourselves to Him on a daily basis, even when life is going smoothly, then at least we can know that God won't have to use trouble and pain to get our attention.

The second truth the Lord makes clear in His reply to the Pharisees is this: People are more important than prejudice. Prejudices are preconceived notions formed before we have sufficient knowledge; they are usually mistaken or distorted ideas we have grown up with. When prejudices come in conflict with real human need, those prejudices must be swept aside without hesitation.

The Christian church has been denounced and abandoned, justifiably so, because of the prejudices it often manifests in terms of class, race, wealth, and gender. If we are to follow truly the example of our Lord, we must become blind to such distinctions. We must treat those who live in the park or on the avenue no differently from those who live on Park Avenue. We must forget who belongs to the white race or the black race or the brown race and remember that there is only one race: the human race. We are all children of the same God. Whenever someone is hungry, hurting, and in need of healing, our job is to be a friend and lead that person to the Great Physician.

I love the words of C. T. Studd, an Englishman who gave away a fortune to serve God in Africa. He expressed his philosophy and the philosophy of the Lord Jesus in these lines:

Some like to dwell
Within the sound
Of church and chapel bell.
But I want to run a rescue shop
Within a yard of Hell.

The Trap of Tradition

The second incident Mark relates in this section deals with the trap of rigid devotion to dead tradition. Mark writes:

> *Now John's disciples and the Pharisees were fasting. Some people came and asked Jesus, "How is it that John's disciples and the disciples of the Pharisees are fasting, but yours are not?"*
>
> *Jesus answered, "How can the guests of the bridegroom fast while he is with them? They cannot, so long as they have him with them. But the time will come when the bridegroom will be taken from them, and on that day they will fast."*
>
> (MARK 2:18–20)

Once again we see a group of offended Pharisees. This event occurred on a day of fasting. The law of Moses required only one day a year to be set aside for fasting, the Day of Atonement (Yom Kippur), which the Jews observe to this day. But over the years, the Pharisees, in an effort to show how righteous and zealous they were, had designated increasingly more and more days as days of fasting. They saw fasting as the best way to call God's attention (and the attention of other people) to their piety. This is why the Pharisees put on sackcloth, rubbed ashes on their faces, and sucked in their cheeks to look gaunt. It was all a religious show to get noticed for their self-righteousness.

This evidently was one of those traditional days of fasting. Some people came to Jesus and said, "Why do John's disciples and the disciples of the Pharisees fast, but your disciples do not fast? Why do you and your disciples flout our traditions and ignore our customs? You should order your disciples to fast!"

Jesus replied, "You've completely misunderstood the nature of the occasion. You think it's a funeral. But no, this is a wedding celebration. The bridegroom is here. No one fasts at a wedding. Everybody feasts! As long as the bridegroom is here, there will be food, festivity, laughter, and rejoicing. There will be plenty of time for fasting when the bridegroom is gone."

This was not just a reply or a rebuke. It was a prophecy. The bridegroom Jesus spoke of was Himself. And He was predicting the coming of the day when He would no longer be among them, when the bridegroom would be taken away and there would be fasting and mourning. From our perspective, two millennia after the crucifixion and resurrection of Christ, we know that there will be times of mourning and sorrow in our lives, but Jesus, the bridegroom, is alive and with us forever. The living presence of Christ in all the situations of our lives turns every day into a feast day.

But Jesus was not just prophesying His coming death. He was also describing the nature of the new relationship He came to bring us. For centuries, the Jews had worshiped in the temple, practicing solemn rituals and slaughtering sacrifices to an unapproachable God. But Jesus told these people of a new relationship of vitality, warmth, and intimacy with the bridegroom, a relationship expressed through joy, gladness, and celebration.

This new, joyful relationship needs to be rediscovered every so often. We lose sight of the reality of relationship, and we fall into the trap of tradition. For centuries, church services have been borrowed from an Old Testament concept of solemn, ritualized worship. This style predominated in the Roman Catholic Church, and it has been carried over unthinkingly into Protestant churches as well. But that is not the image of worship Jesus presents. He says that worship is to be a feast, not a fast; a time of celebration, not solemnity.

No wonder the world dismisses the church as boring, irrelevant, and unreal. Church as it has often been practiced is morbidly traditional and deadly dull. Until the church recovers the excitement and joy of a wedding feast, until people are glad to be at church instead of depressed about it, you cannot blame people for staying away. When the church recovers the sense of feasting and celebration that Jesus indicates here, people will stream into our worship services. They will find the joy of the Lord there, and they will say, "It is good to be in the house of the Lord!"

The New Versus the Old

Jesus underscores the difference between feasting and fasting, celebrating and sorrowing, with two vivid word pictures.

> *"No one sews a patch of unshrunk cloth on an old garment. If he does, the new piece will pull away from the old, making the tear worse. And no one pours new wine into old wineskins. If he does, the wine will burst the skins, and both the wine and the wineskins will be ruined. No, he pours new wine into new wineskins."* (MARK 2:21–22)

Jesus was a master at illustrating concepts. "No one sews a patch of unshrunk cloth on an old garment," He says. In other words, "When you have a joyful, celebratory relationship with me, that is no time to patch up the old with the new." Fresh, new relationships require new expressions. When a relationship becomes old, stale, and tiresome, the quality of that relationship deteriorates. The warmth and joy depart. But then, when the relationship experiences a new awakening, do not try to express it through the old forms. It will not work. The new is too powerful and will destroy those old forms that try to contain it.

We have an example of this in the way many churches are coming alive these days with a fresh awakening of the Spirit. And what happens to those newly awakened churches? New forms of worship replace the old rituals. A new spirit of celebration replaces the old solemnity. New forms of musical and dramatic expression sweep through the church. Hands that once were folded quietly in a solemn pose of piety are now raised joyfully or clapping loudly. New people, new faces, and new ideas flood the church, transforming the congregation.

When Christ comes into a church as a living person rather than a stained-glass image, then old things are passed away, and all things are made new. Jesus wants us to avoid the error of putting an unshrunk patch onto a new garment. As the patch shrinks, it tears a hole larger than before.

The second illustration is parallel to the first. "No one pours new wine into old wineskins. If he does, the wine will burst the skins, and both the wine and the wineskins will be ruined. No, he pours new wine into new wineskins." People did not have bottles in those days. Instead, they bottled wine in sewn-up animal skins. The old ones became brittle and inflexible and would burst easily if filled with new wine. Why? Because new wine is still fermenting and giving off gases, which make the wineskin expand like a balloon. If you put bubbling new wine into brittle old wineskins, the skins will burst and the wine will be lost.

Wine is the symbol of joy and celebration. Jesus was telling His listeners that if you pour the joy and celebration of a new, living relationship with God into a container that is old, rigid, dried out, and brittle, the old container will burst. It cannot contain the effervescence of the new relationship. Wineskins must be flexible to hold new wine. And people and religious structures must be flexible in order to contain the exciting new relationship Jesus brings. They cannot be rigid and unyielding, or the new wine of the new relationship will be lost.

Our Lord, in His great wisdom, shows us what happens when groups and individuals suddenly discover a new and vital relationship with Him. They must find new ways to express it and embody it. The old ways will not do. The message Jesus imparted two thousand years ago is the same message we need to hear and receive in these days. If we are to express and embody the joyful celebration of a living relationship with Christ, we must not try to contain it within old structures, old forms, old rituals, old ideas, and old attitudes. The new has come, and we must be new and flexible in order to receive it.

So beware the trap of tradition. The attitude that says, "This is how we've always done it," is deadly to vibrant, exciting relationships with God and with others. Jesus fought rigid, confining tradition in His day, and we, as His followers, must fight it in our day, in our lives, and our churches. We must become gentle subversives, always at war against those traditions that would stifle the reality of a living relationship with God and with one another.

Rules Made to be Broken

The third incident Mark describes has to do with the problem of rules. He writes:

> *One Sabbath Jesus was going through the grainfields, and as his disciples walked along, they began to pick some heads of grain. The Pharisees said to him, "Look, why are they doing what is unlawful on the Sabbath?"*
>
> *He answered, "Have you never read what David did when he and his companions were hungry and in need? In the days of Abiathar the high priest, he entered the house of God and ate the consecrated bread, which is lawful only for priests to eat. And he also gave some to his companions."*
>
> *Then he said to them, "The Sabbath was made for man, not man for the Sabbath. So the Son of Man is Lord even of the Sabbath."* (MARK 2:23–28)

Again Jesus places Himself in direct confrontation with the Pharisees. His disciples had been doing what was proper on any weekday. They were not stealing from the farmer, for the law said that any passing travelers could thresh out a few heads of grain in their hands and eat the wheat as long as they did not put a sickle to the grain. The only problem was that the disciples were picking heads of grain on the Sabbath. By the time of Christ, the religious leaders had placed 1,001 restrictions and rules on the Sabbath.

We must remember God's purpose in establishing the Sabbath. It was originally given to restore men and women, to ensure that they had a healthy amount of rest and spiritual reflection each week. Thoughtfully observed, the Sabbath should have been a day of joy, but the Pharisees had so encumbered the Sabbath with human rules that they had made it a burden instead.

Look at one example among hundreds. The Pharisees held that it was acceptable to spit on a rock on the Sabbath, but if you spit on the ground, that made mud. Mud is mortar for bricklaying. If you spit on the ground and made mortar, you were working on the Sabbath. So it was forbidden to spit on the ground. That gives you an idea of how ridiculous the Sabbath restrictions were. In a similar fashion, the Pharisees saw Jesus' disciples picking a head of grain on the Sabbath to ease their hunger, but to the Pharisees, the disciples were harvesting on the day of rest.

When Jesus answered the Pharisees, however, He skewered them on their own sword, which was the Scripture. They were supporting their regulations and defending their laws by the commandment, "Remember the Sabbath day by keeping it holy. Six days you shall labor and do all your work, but the seventh day is a Sabbath to the LORD your God" (Exodus 20:8–10).

But Jesus said, "Wait a minute. Have you never read 1 Samuel 21? David and his men, fleeing for their lives, were hungry. There was no ordinary food available, so in desperation they entered the tabernacle, went into the holy place, took the showbread, which God had said was designated for the priests only, and ate it. Twelve loaves of bread, standing as a symbol for Israel, prepared fresh each week, were placed on the table in the tabernacle. By law, the priests, and only the priests, could eat it. But David, because of the hunger of his men, dared to go in and take those loaves of bread and pass them out among them. And God did not punish David and his men. Now what do you make of that?"

The Pharisees had no reply.

So Jesus drew this conclusion for them: "The Sabbath was made for man, not man for the Sabbath. So the Son of Man is

Lord even of the Sabbath." With these words, He underscored the principle that should govern our lives as believers: Human need always takes precedence over rules. Hunger is healthy and therefore holy. It is wrong to make rules that prevent people from satisfying the basic needs of their lives.

It is easy to focus on a single act and say, "You can't do that! It's against the rules!" But what is the purpose of the rules? To make life orderly, happy, and healthy. When the rules create disharmony, unhappiness, and misery, then the rules no longer serve us. Instead, human beings are turned into slaves of the rules. That is the principle Jesus forced the religious leaders to examine. The Sabbath was made to restore people, but when the Sabbath became a burden and a hindrance, then the rules needed to be changed.

Our church once sent a ministry team to a Christian college in the Midwest. We held a worship meeting in a large room in the women's dormitory, where there was a 10:30 P.M. curfew. God broke through in a remarkable way during that meeting, and the young people began to celebrate together, laugh together, weep together, confess wrongs and forgive one another, and pray for one another. It was a great movement of the Spirit of God.

Promptly at curfew, the dorm mother appeared with a glower on her face that was as dark and threatening as a thunderstorm. "It is ten-thirty," she announced, "and time for these girls to be in their rooms!"

"But God is working here," said a member of our ministry team, "and surely you don't want to stand in the way of what God is doing in these kids' lives tonight."

"Rules are rules," the woman replied, "and I'm the dorm mother here. It's my job to see that the rules are followed!"

At that, another member of our ministry team was struck by an inspiration, no doubt directly from the Lord. "Well," he said kindly and gently, "we certainly understand your situation. How about if you and I step into that room over there and discuss the matter. I'm sure we can come to some sort of an understanding." And he guided the dorm mother into another room, where they talked for more than two hours.

By the time they emerged from the room, the meeting had come to a wonderful conclusion, and the young people had all gone off to their rooms with hearts full of blessing and rejoicing.

All too often, we are like that dorm mother. "Rules are rules!" we say. But Jesus has come to show us that human need takes precedence over rules. The purpose of rules is to provide an orderly way of meeting human need. But when the rules hinder that purpose, the rules must go. That is the principle Jesus makes clear in this passage.

Growing Hostility

The final incident Mark records deals with the danger of zealous pride. Mark writes:

> Another time [Jesus] went into the synagogue, and a man with a shriveled hand was there. Some of them were looking for a reason to accuse Jesus, so they watched him closely to see if he would heal him on the Sabbath. Jesus said to the man with the shriveled hand, "Stand up in front of everyone."
>
> Then Jesus asked them, "Which is lawful on the Sabbath: to do good or to do evil, to save life or to kill?" But they remained silent.
>
> He looked around at them in anger and, deeply distressed at their stubborn hearts, said to the man, "Stretch out your hand." He stretched it out, and his hand was completely

restored. Then the Pharisees went out and began to plot with
the Herodians how they might kill Jesus. (MARK 3:1–6)

Here is a crucial moment in the ministry of Jesus, marking
the climax of a growing hostility that can be traced in the increasingly belligerent questions asked by the Pharisees. The first question they asked was seemingly innocuous: "Why does he eat with
tax collectors and 'sinners'?" The second has more of the tone of
an accusation: "How is it that John's disciples and the disciples of
the Pharisees are fasting, but yours are not?" The third is an
aggressive, abrasive indictment of Jesus, an indictment for breaking the law: "Look, why are they doing what is unlawful on the
Sabbath?" In this passage, we see that the Pharisees are waiting
to ambush and entrap Jesus. The fourth brings before us this
statement: "Some of them were looking for a reason to accuse
Jesus, so they watched him closely." The hostility is sharpened,
the synagogue door is closing to Jesus, and the Pharisees have
become His avowed enemies.

Yet, at the same time, Jesus' enemies paid Him a remarkable
compliment. When He went into the synagogue, they followed
Him closely, knowing that a man was there with a withered hand.
They knew that on entering, Jesus would see the man and have
compassion for him. It was a tribute to His character that even
Jesus' enemies knew His heart. They knew that His heart of love
would not be closed against a man in need, and so they hoped to
use His compassion against Him in order to trap Him.

Notice how Jesus handled the situation. If His enemies
sought to trap Him, He would respond by flushing them into the
open. He wouldn't try to hide His act of compassion for the man
with the withered arm. No, He would turn a spotlight on the
man. It was as if Jesus was saying, "I don't want any of you to miss

this. Come here and watch!" As the man stood in the midst of them, Jesus turned to the Pharisees and asked two penetrating questions.

Here, as I would paraphrase it, is the first question He asked as He read their thoughts and intentions: "You're concerned about the Sabbath, aren't you? Let me ask you: Whose thoughts are nearer to the purpose of the Sabbath—yours or mine? I want to do good to this man, while you want to harm me. I want to save this man and heal him; you're thinking of killing me. Now, which is in line with the purpose of the Sabbath?" Mark says they were silent. None of them had an answer. And no wonder!

Then, angered at their hardness of heart, Jesus turned and healed the man. His healing response underscores a key principle: When people become overly zealous in enforcing rules and regulations, they usually invalidate the purpose of those rules and regulations. The Sabbath was a good thing, given to humanity by God. But in their zeal, these religious leaders had so overruled and overregulated the Sabbath that they had turned God's beautiful gift into a travesty. The purpose of the Sabbath was to free people from work and drudgery for a day, so they could focus on God; instead, it became a straightjacket that confined and imprisoned the people. The Pharisees' zeal to honor and maintain the Sabbath had ruined and perverted it.

Jesus exposed the evil result of their zeal, their rules and regulations, and their plot to entrap Him. Mark records that their immediate reaction was one of rage—so much blind, unreasoning rage that they went out and joined their enemies, the Herodians, in plotting to kill Jesus. Why did Jesus deliberately provoke controversy and hostility and ultimately a murder plot?

We all know people who are controversial for the sake of stirring up controversy. But Jesus was not that kind of person. Notice that in all of His answers to the Pharisees, He was never threatening or attacking or insulting. His words were skillful, subtle, and precisely targeted like a laser-guided missile, but He was always gracious, never rude or abrasive. He offended people, but never for the sake of offending, only for the sake of teaching people and accomplishing His mission in the world.

Although He was neither aggressive nor abrasive, Jesus was fearless. He never compromised or backed away from controversy and confrontation. One principle governed His words and deeds: He was true to the truth. He refused to let ridiculous rules, petty traditions, intolerant prejudices, and excessive zeal stand in His way of doing what God had sent Him to do.

With Jesus as our model, may we follow in His footsteps, shattering the oppressive and confining attitudes, traditions, structures, rules, and regulations that hold people in bondage. Jesus never hesitated to cause a scandal when He could heal hurting people and set captives free. He scandalized the oppressors. They turned on Him and plotted His death.

May we have the courage to follow His example, daring opposition, braving controversy, defying tradition and prejudice, creating scandals of love, joy, and celebration wherever we go. May we be Christian scandal makers, walking in the footsteps of the great scandal maker, our Lord Jesus Christ.

SIX

False Forces

➤ **Mark 3:7–35**

The life of Jesus has been portrayed many times and in various ways in motion pictures. Although Jesus was the focus of the 1953 film *The Robe,* we never see His face in the film, and we hear Him speak only a few words, such as His cry from the cross, "My God, my God, why hast thou forsaken me?" It is a sign of reverence on the part of the filmmaker, who knows that no depiction, no actor, no script can possibly do justice to the historic reality of God-made-man, Jesus Christ. The same reverence is shown for Jesus in William Wyler's *Ben Hur* (1959), which shows Jesus' hands or feet but not His face.

Films that attempted to depict Jesus directly, such as *King of Kings* (1961) and *The Greatest Story Ever Told* (1965), seem to lose their focus amid the dramatic subplots and Hollywood stars that were so much a part of the biblical screen epics of that era. The simple message of the Christian gospel tends to get lost in the various Tinseltown versions. Some films, such as Italian Marxist director Pier Paolo Pasolini's *The Gospel According to St. Matthew* (1964), are slanted to produce an image of Jesus as a political revolutionary. Others, like Norman Jewison's *Jesus Christ Superstar* (1973), seem intent on robbing Jesus of His identity as God, portraying Him as just a man, a Palestinian wonder worker who gets too carried away with His celebrity status.

Given the many interpretations and versions of Jesus that have been imprinted on our consciousness by Hollywood, it is important that we return to the source documents, the four gospels. Each reveals a different facet of the nature and character of Jesus. The emphasis of Mark's gospel is on that beautiful balance between Jesus' roles as God and man. Mark reveals to us the wonderful picture of the Servant who rules and the Ruler who serves.

Jesus' Mission—Hindered by Success?

At this point in Mark's gospel, we come to the third division of the story. The first division, Mark 1:1–39, portrays the theme of the authority of the Servant, the tremendous command Jesus exercised in many realms. The second division, Mark 1:40–3:6, portrays His knowledge of our humanity, the penetrating, incisive understanding of human beings that Jesus exhibited. The third division of this gospel, Mark 3:7–6:6, portrays for us the immense popularity of our Lord and His ministry. This theme is introduced in the opening paragraph of this division.

> *Jesus withdrew with his disciples to the lake, and a large crowd from Galilee followed. When they heard all he was doing, many people came to him from Judea, Jerusalem, Idumea, and the regions across the Jordan and around Tyre and Sidon.* (MARK 3:7–8)

How large was this crowd? It numbered not just in the hundreds or thousands. There were literally tens of thousands of people in this crowd. They came from all over the region: from Galilee, from Judea, from the Judean capital of Jerusalem some seventy miles to the south, from the land of Idumea (or Edom) in the southern desert, from the desert east of the Jordan River, from the west all the way to the Mediterranean coast and up the coast to Tyre and Sidon (modern Lebanon). People from all these cities flocked to hear this amazing prophet who had arisen in Galilee and was doing and saying such startling things.

Mark will underscore the size of the crowds throughout this account. In Mark 3:20, he writes that the press of the crowd is so great that Jesus and His disciples cannot even eat. In Mark 4:1, the crowd presses in on Jesus as He teaches beside the sea. In Mark 5:21, Jesus crosses in a boat to the other side of the sea, and again He is besieged by crowds. Everywhere He goes, the crowds follow Him, crush against Him, shout at Him, and plead with Him. It is difficult to imagine how exhausting and draining those crowds must have been for Him.

You might think that the crowds are a symbol of Jesus' success. Anyone who can build a great following today is regarded as successful and is called a celebrity or a superstar. That is why a popular musical in the 1970s, portraying Jesus as a victim of His celebrity status, was called *Jesus Christ Superstar.*

But as you read through Mark's account, you get a different picture of Jesus' success. Mark's intention is to underscore the emptiness of popularity, the worthlessness and even danger of celebrity status. In three specific ways, Mark underscores the damage that Jesus' burgeoning popularity does to His ministry and mission in the world. This is no small point. It is relevant to our experience. It is a warning to us.

In this division of Mark's gospel, we will see the hindrance that so easily arises whenever a person or a movement becomes popular. We will see three different false forces of seeming success that can drag an individual or a ministry into ruin.

The First False Force: Misguided Expectations and Emphases

Mark introduces us to the first danger, that of popularity. After describing the crowd, Mark writes:

> *Because of the crowd he told his disciples to have a small boat ready for him, to keep the people from crowding him. For he had healed many, so that those with diseases were pushing forward to touch him.* (MARK 3:9–10)

The crowd's imagination focused on false expectations and false emphases. Misunderstanding the purpose for which Jesus came, they concentrated on a secondary aspect of His ministry: physical healings. But that was not preeminently what Jesus came to do. In fact, as you read the gospels, you see that Jesus continually downplays the issue of physical healings. The purpose of physical healings was to demonstrate what He could do in the realm of the spirit. Physical healings were object lessons of that true and lasting form of healing He came to bring us.

The crowd misunderstood Jesus' purpose. They pressed in on Him so that He might touch those who were sick and heal them. As a result, Jesus had to resort to a stratagem to avoid being crushed by the crowd. He had His disciples keep a boat handy so that He could move out onto the lake, where the crowd couldn't follow Him. His primary purpose was to preach, not to heal.

The Second False Force: The Rise of Unclean Spirits

Another false force, the force of unclean spirits or demons, arises in response to Jesus' rising popularity. Mark writes:

> *Whenever the evil spirits saw him, they fell down before him and cried out, "You are the Son of God."* (MARK 3:11)

Many people came to Jesus for healing from physical disease. And the Scriptures tell us that behind many diseases is a malevolent presence and power—the power of demons. Have you noticed how many times the Bible refers to demons as "unclean spirits"? One of the ways you can recognize the presence of a demon is that it is unclean, either physically or morally.

A friend once told me that he knew a man who had an unclean spirit. As they talked in a hotel room, the man placed his hat on the bed. When he left, my friend found a ring of foul-smelling grease where the hat had been. The odor pervaded the room for days, a reminder of the uncleanness of that spirit.

I once talked to a girl who had fallen into the practice of using an Ouija board. She eventually began to hear voices that demanded she write things before she could sleep at night. Invariably the things she was ordered to write involved moral filth, obscenities, blasphemies, and evil words. Sometimes she would have to write pages of them before the voices would cease and she could sleep. That is clear evidence of an unclean spirit.

Mark tells us that when the demons saw Jesus, they identified Him. They cried out, "You are the Son of God!" And Jesus invariably silenced them and cast them out. Why do you suppose He rejected this testimony from the demons? What they said was true, wasn't it?

In Acts 16, Paul and Silas were preaching in Philippi. As they walked the streets of the city, they were followed by a slave girl who made money for her owners by telling fortunes. She cried out after them, "These men are servants of the Most High God, who are telling you the way to be saved." It was a true testimony that she gave, but Paul and Silas refused her witness. Finally Paul turned and said, "In the name of Jesus Christ I command you to come out of her!" And the unclean spirit left her. Throughout the

Scriptures, Jesus and His apostles rejected testimony that came from an unclean, demonic source, even when that testimony was accurate. Why?

We can be sure of one thing. These unclean spirits were not trying to advance the cause of Christ by their witness. Even though they spoke accurately, they didn't speak the truth. Instead, they used accurate facts to mislead and to exploit people and to hinder the gospel.

In a scene near the end of the film *Absence of Malice,* two reporters are discussing the facts of a newspaper story. One reporter asks the other, Megan Carter, played by Sally Field, "Is that the truth?" Megan Carter replies, "No, but it's accurate."

You see, what is accurate is not always the truth. Accurate facts are often used by people and demons to create a false or destructive impression. That is what the demons do in announcing Jesus to the people. What they say is accurate, but they oppose the truth, especially the truth of the gospel of Jesus Christ. So Jesus rejects their testimony, silences them, and casts them out.

At the same time, it is important to understand the cultural context in which these demons made their announcements. To the first-century Jewish listener, the term "son of God" did not necessarily mean what it means to us: the only begotten Son of the Father, the second person of the Trinity. To them, that term could mean a created but powerful being, such as Satan. And it is likely that these demons intended people to believe that Jesus was the "son of God" whom the demons worshiped, that is, Satan. This would help explain why, in Mark 3:22, some teachers of the law of Moses arrive from Jerusalem, accusing Jesus of being possessed by the prince of demons. If word had been passed to these teachers of the law that demons were praising

Jesus as a "son of God," they may well have taken this to mean that Jesus was inhabited by Satan.

How did Jesus deal with the hindrance of those unclean spirits? Mark records that He took action. He called the Twelve and chose them as apostles. You may wonder what the calling of the Twelve has to do with combating demons. Read what Mark records:

> *Jesus went up on a mountainside and called to him those he wanted, and they came to him. He appointed twelve—designating them apostles—that they might be with him and that he might send them out to preach and to have authority to drive out demons. These are the twelve he appointed: Simon (to whom he gave the name Peter); James son of Zebedee and his brother John (to them he gave the name Boanerges, which means Sons of Thunder); Andrew, Philip, Bartholomew, Matthew, Thomas, James son of Alphaeus, Thaddaeus, Simon the Zealot and Judas Iscariot, who betrayed him.* (MARK 3:13–19)

These are the Twelve Jesus selected. Mark contrasts this paragraph and the preceding one to show that Jesus did not want pretentious claims and impressive titles from demons, accurate as they might have been. Rather, the testimony He sought was the witness of changed lives and empowered words. So He chose men and sent them out to tell what they had heard and learned from Him, and He gave them the power to speak with authority, including authority over demons. That is the witness He chose then, and it is the witness He still chooses.

These twelve men were called to do perform three tasks, as Mark describes them.

"That they might be with him." The Twelve were called to a personal experience with Jesus. Our Lord never wants anyone to talk about Christianity merely as a salesman but as a witness, someone who has experienced what he is talking about. A mere salesman can make a pitch on behalf of Christianity; he can sing the jingle and recite the slogan. But only an experiencer can be a witness.

"And that he might send them out to preach." They were sent out as preachers, as evangelists. They were sent out to tell what they had learned from Him.

"And to have authority to drive out demons." They were given power over unclean spirits.

In other words, the Twelve were given something to say, they were sent out to say it, and they were given power over all opposition.

It is significant that Jesus selected only twelve men to reach a multitude. As it turns out, He knew what He was doing. We make a great mistake by relying too heavily on mass media and sophisticated marketing techniques. We think we are going to reach the multitudes through all the great inventions that have come along—radio, television, audiotapes, videotapes, the Internet, and more. As helpful as these mass media may be, they will never take the place of men and women who have had a personal experience with Christ and who tell their story at every opportunity. People may tell their stories via one of those media channels; however, the power is not in the medium but in the message of a life that has been changed by a relationship with Jesus Christ.

Mark lists the names of the twelve disciples, and those names are probably familiar to you. Simon, James, and John are listed first, and they were all given special names by Jesus. This marks them as belonging to an inner circle within the Twelve.

Whenever Jesus had an especially important or burdensome task, He took the inner circle with Him—Peter, James, and John. He dealt more intimately with these three than with any of the others. He marked them as leaders of the group of twelve. To Simon, He gave the name Peter, or Rock. James and John He called the Sons of Thunder. Those names proved to be prophetic. Peter became the acknowledged leader of the Twelve, the steady one to whom the others looked for leadership and sound guidance. Oh, yes, he would fail his first big test the night before the crucifixion, but he would ultimately prove himself a rock after the resurrection, when he assumed leadership in the early Christian church.

James and John served as the bookends of the apostles. James was the first to be martyred and John the last. Between the death of James and the death of John, the apostolic witness was delivered. James left his mark by setting an example for all the martyrs who followed. John remained until the end to gather up all the apostolic witness, solidify it, and transmit it to us in its final expression in the gospel of John, the three letters of John, and the book of Revelation.

So this was the leadership circle within the Twelve. Like a Marine Corps recruiter, Jesus recruited "a few good men," and He was content to work with them and mold them into His apostles, His witnesses.

The Third False Force: Misunderstanding on All Sides
The mushrooming popularity of Jesus gave rise to yet another false force that Mark introduces to us with these words:

> *Then Jesus entered a house, and again a crowd gathered,*
> *so that he and his disciples were not even able to eat. When*

his family heard about this, they went to take charge of him, for they said, "He is out of his mind."

And the teachers of the law who came down from Jerusalem said, "He is possessed by Beelzebub! By the prince of demons he is driving out demons." (MARK 3:20–22)

Here we see two reactions to Jesus as a result of the rapid growth of His ministry.

First, He was misunderstood by His family. Jesus gave Himself so totally to this ministry that He had no time even to eat. His family heard about this (in the latter part of the chapter, we learn that it was His mother and brothers). Word reached them that Jesus was exhausting Himself in ministry to the crowds. He wasn't eating or sleeping properly, and His health was threatened. So they left Nazareth and came to place Him under restraint. They believed He was out of His mind from the pressures of the hurting people who crowded around Him. Later in this account, we will see how Jesus dealt with His family's misunderstanding of His ministry and mission in the world.

Second, He was misunderstood by the teachers of the law who came from Jerusalem and watched Him at work. They saw Him casting out demons, and their explanation was, "He is possessed by the devil, by Beelzebub." Beelzebub means "lord of the house." It was a reference to Satan as king of the underworld, as head of the demonic mafia. Beelzebub was the godfather who gave orders to the rest of demonkind. The scribes' explanation of Jesus' ministry was that He was in league with the devil, that He had joined the demonic mafia and was casting out demons by the power of the satanic godfather.

But their conclusion was illogical, as Jesus demonstrated in His response.

So Jesus called them and spoke to them in parables: "How can Satan drive out Satan? If a kingdom is divided against itself, that kingdom cannot stand. If a house is divided against itself, that house cannot stand. And if Satan opposes himself and is divided, he cannot stand; his end has come." (MARK 3:23–26)

The logic of Jesus is unassailable. Why, Jesus asks, would Satan cast out Satan? Why would Satan undermine himself? It makes no sense. Satan is crafty and resourceful, not stupid. Satan is not going to oppose himself. His plan is to create division between God and people and between people and people. It is not the power of Satan that casts out demons, but another power altogether. What power is that? Jesus answers with another example.

"In fact, no one can enter a strong man's house and carry off his possessions unless he first ties up the strong man. Then he can rob his house." (MARK 3:27)

Who is the "strong man" Jesus talks about? Satan. But, Jesus says, if an even stronger man enters the strong man's house and ties up the strong man, he can rob the house. Who is the stronger man Jesus alludes to? It is Jesus! Jesus, the stronger man, has entered the house of Satan and has bound him. That is why Jesus was able to cast out demons. As the stronger man, He has bound Satan, and Satan is powerless to prevent Him from tossing the demons of hell out on their ears.

Some people talk about binding Satan. But I submit that it is unnecessary to bind Satan. Only one "stronger man" can bind the devil, and He has already done so. Jesus bound the devil in the days of His ministry, and this enabled Him to plunder the house of Satan and cast out unclean spirits. In doing so, Jesus released those who had been held captive for so long under Satan's dominion: all of humanity. This is what Jesus did. So we don't need to bind the devil; we need only exercise the authority that is ours to cast out unclean spirits.

A Severe Warning

Having answered the charge against Him, Jesus issues a severe warning to these teachers of the law.

> *"I tell you the truth, all the sins and blasphemies of men will be forgiven them. But whoever blasphemes against the Holy Spirit will never be forgiven; he is guilty of an eternal sin." He said this because they were saying, "He has an evil spirit."* (MARK 3:28–30)

Many readers have been frightened by that paragraph, and rightly so. It is a serious warning. Some people have concluded from this warning that the unpardonable sin involves accusing Jesus of having an unclean spirit or suggesting that the works of God are really the works of the devil. But it is important to notice certain things about this account. First, these men had not yet committed the unpardonable sin when they said Jesus had an unclean spirit. Otherwise Jesus would never have warned them. By His own words, there is no use warning a man who has committed the unpardonable sin; he is beyond help. So, if that is what these men had done, there would have been no point to His warning. But Jesus did warn them, so it is clear that they had not yet committed this sin.

But they are on the verge of committing the unpardonable sin. "You are very close to committing that sin," Jesus says, in effect, "when you ascribe the work of God to the devil." What

Jesus warned them against was rejecting the witness of the Holy Spirit. And of whom does the Spirit witness? The Lord Jesus.

We see it all through Scripture: "When the Counselor comes, whom I will send to you from the Father, the Spirit of truth who goes out from the Father, he will testify about me" (John 15:26). Jesus said later to His disciples, "He [the Spirit] will bring glory to me by taking from what is mine and making it known to you" (John 16:14). He came into the world to "convict the world of guilt in regard to sin and righteousness and judgment: in regard to sin, because men do not believe in me" (John 16:8–9). All the work of the Holy Spirit is designed to exalt and declare the work of Jesus. To reject the Holy Spirit's witness of Christ is to blaspheme the Holy Spirit.

That is what these men were close to doing. And if there is ultimately a rejection of Christ, then there is no hope, because there is no ground of forgiveness other than faith in the Lord Jesus. People are forgiven when they believe in His name and on no other basis. If the heart is resistant and rejects the claims of Jesus as set forth by the Spirit, there can be no forgiveness. This is Scripture's sharp way of underscoring what Jesus declared: "I am the way and the truth and the life. No one comes to the Father except through me" (John 14:6).

Jesus Answers His Family
Next our Lord deals with the misunderstanding that arises from His family.

> *Then Jesus' mother and brothers arrived. Standing outside, they sent someone in to call him. A crowd was sitting around him, and they told him, "Your mother and brothers are outside looking for you."*

"Who are my mother and my brothers?" he asked.

Then he looked at those seated in a circle around him
and said, "Here are my mother and my brothers! Whoever
does God's will is my brother and sister and mother."

(MARK 3:31–35)

When word was brought in that Jesus' mother and brothers were outside, everyone expected Him to immediately go out and see them. But Jesus didn't, and this was a deliberate decision. Instead of going out to His family, He looked around and said these strange words: "Here are my mother and my brothers! Whoever does God's will is my brother and sister and mother." In other words, "Whoever does the will of God is even closer to me than my family."

Was Jesus mentally unbalanced because He seemingly neglected His family and even neglected His needs? No, He simply recognized a stronger tie, a deeper relationship than the genetic bond. His relationships in the family of God were dearer to Him than even His earthly family. Blood may be thicker than water, as the saying goes, but the Spirit of God trumps even blood.

At this point, a word of caution is in order. Jesus is not saying that we should abandon family. Nor is He abrogating the command given by God in Exodus 20:12: "Honor your father and your mother, so that you may live long in the land the LORD your God is giving you." Respect and honor are always to be given to our family members, and especially to parents. Jesus never teaches us to ignore our family responsibilities. As Paul makes clear in 1 Timothy 5:8, "If anyone does not provide for his relatives, and especially for his immediate family, he has denied the faith and is worse than an unbeliever."

Later, in Mark 7 (see also Matthew 15), we will examine a story in which the Pharisees try to trap Jesus, accusing Him of breaking their tradition. Jesus turns the tables on them, asking, "Why do you break God's command just to keep your human tradition? God said, 'Honor your father and mother.' Yet you rationalize letting your parents be hungry, needy, and destitute—as long as you are giving donations to the temple. You hypocrites! Isaiah was right when he said of you, 'These people honor me with their lips, but their hearts are far from me. They worship me in vain; their teachings are but rules taught by men.'" Jesus makes it clear that there is no excuse for neglecting parents, not even the excuse of giving to God. If you claim to be devoted to God but you neglect your parents, you are nothing but a hypocrite.

But what if a parent's wishes conflict with God's Word? Do we have to honor what that parent says? Clearly not. Whenever there is a conflict between what God says and what a parent says, we must obey God. We must obey His Word over the word of any human being, including parents. If we must confront or say no to a parent, we can still show godly honor by stating our decision with love, respect, and understanding: "I'm sorry, Mom, but I cannot tell a lie to protect you, because God's command against lying takes precedence." Or, "Dad, I know you told me not to confront you about your unfaithfulness to Mom, but God's law takes precedence."

With this perspective, it becomes clear to us why Jesus made such statements as this: "If anyone comes to me and does not hate his father and mother, his wife and children, his brothers and sisters—yes, even his own life—he cannot be my disciple" (Luke 14:26). Jesus makes that supreme claim on us, having fulfilled it Himself. And this is why He seems to ignore His ties with His mother and siblings; He did not dishonor His family, but first and foremost, He had to be faithful to the calling of God.

The Snare of Popularity

These, then, are the three false forces that can entangle us when we become popular and successful as individuals or as a movement. People will have misguided expectations about us and emphasize the wrong aspects of our ministry, as when the people sought Jesus' healing so much that it hindered His preaching. Our ministry will come under satanic attack, as Jesus experienced when the unclean spirits announced that He was the "son of God." There will be misunderstanding on all sides, not only from our opponents but even from family and friends.

In this section of his gospel, Mark underscores an important truth. Popularity is empty and meaningless; celebrity status is dangerous and can even hinder our mission. Fame quickly gives rise to dangerous forces that will destroy us if we do not rely on God's power from moment to moment, just as Jesus did. It is not wrong to be famous, nor is it wrong for a Christian movement to become popular. But we must be careful and on our guard. Amid the noise of the crowd, we must continually listen to that still, small voice of the Spirit of God.

seven

The Dimming of the Light

➤ **Mark 4:1–12, 21–25, 33–34**

I have heard the comics pages referred to as the theological section of the newspaper. And it is true that a number of newspaper cartoonists, such as Bil Keane ("Family Circus"), Johnny Hart ("B.C."), and Charles Schulz ("Peanuts"), have used their comic strips as an entertaining pulpit for discussing Christian faith and values. Robert L. Short, author of *The Gospel According to Peanuts* (New York: Bantam, 1968) called Schulz's classic comic strip "a modern-day Christian parable." Like the parables of Jesus, the visual parables of Charles Schulz make a subtle point but leave the interpretation of the story up to the listener.

In one "Peanuts" installment, Linus and Charlie Brown got into an argument about the Great Pumpkin versus Santa Claus. As was often the case, Schulz wanted to evoke more than just a laugh; he wanted his readers to catch a glimpse of truth about the nature of faith. As the argument between Linus and Charlie Brown grows more heated, Linus finally gets frustrated and says, "All right, so you believe in Santa Claus, and I believe in the Great Pumpkin! The way I see it, it doesn't matter what you believe just as long as you're sincere."

In another "Peanuts" strip, Schulz depicted Linus building an elaborate sand castle at the beach. Moments after he completes the sand castle, an ocean wave washes over it, obliterating Linus's work—reminiscent of the Lord's words in Matthew 7:26: "Everyone who hears these words of mine and does not put them into practice is like a foolish man who built his house on sand." As Linus laments in the last panel of the strip, "I know there's a lesson in this somewhere, but I can't remember what it is."

The parables of "Peanuts," "Family Circus," and "B.C." are part of a great tradition of teaching that goes back to Jesus. Most of His teaching was in parable form, that is, in little stories that illustrate great truths. Jesus used these oral cartoons to make vivid, memorable impressions of truth on the minds of those who heard Him. In this section of Mark's gospel, we will watch Jesus as He communicates profound, eternal truths compressed into unforgettable word pictures.

A New Way of Teaching

As we move into Mark 4, we see that Mark is still dealing with the theme of the previous chapter: the danger of popularity. The Lord is beset by multitudes. He is besieged by satanic opposition from unclean spirits. And now we examine what I call the dimming of the light, a subtler and less direct form of teaching made necessary by Jesus' growing popularity. I call parables a dimming of the light because they make their points gently and indirectly instead of boldly, as a direct statement would. Here is how Mark describes the situation:

> *Again Jesus began to teach by the lake. The crowd that gathered around him was so large that he got into a boat and sat in it out on the lake, while all the people were along the shore at the water's edge. He taught them many things by parables . . . .* (MARK 4:1–2)

This opening comment takes us back to Mark 3, where the great multitude is described to us. They came from Judea, Jerusalem, Idumea, beyond the Jordan, and the Mediterranean region of Tyre and Sidon. We need to remember why this crowd had come. They were looking for healing. They had brought the sick in great numbers to Jesus, and He healed many people, even though physical healing was not His primary mission.

As He did in Mark 3, Jesus has prepared an emergency exit in the event that the crowds press in too closely. He has a boat ready, which He enters. The boat is pushed out from shore, and He proceeds to preach to the people on the shore from the safety of the water. As He preaches, He begins to teach in a new way, through little stories called parables. This is the first time Jesus uses parables, and the first story He tells (all the gospel accounts agree on this) is the parable of the sower. As they listen, the twelve disciples are impressed by this story and by the way Jesus tells it. Here is Mark's account.

> *He taught them many things by parables, and in his teaching said: "Listen! A farmer went out to sow his seed. As he was scattering the seed, some fell along the path, and the birds came and ate it up. Some fell on rocky places, where it did not have much soil. It sprang up quickly, because the soil was shallow. But when the sun came up, the plants were scorched, and they withered because they had no root. Other seed fell among thorns, which grew up and choked the plants, so that they did not bear grain. Still other seed fell on good soil. It came up, grew and produced a crop, multiplying thirty, sixty, or even a hundred times."*
>
> *Then Jesus said, "He who has ears to hear, let him hear."*
> (Mark 4:2–9)

In this section, the parable of the sower is linked with two other stories of seeds. There is the parable of the secretly growing grain (Mark 4:26–29) and the parable of the mustard seed (Mark 4:30–32). We will examine those stories in the next chapter. For now, let's focus on the parable of the sower, the story that aroused the disciples' curiosity as to why Jesus taught in parables. The disciples ask Him about the parables, and He explains.

> *When he was alone, the Twelve and the others around him asked him about the parables. He told them, "The secret of the kingdom of God has been given to you. But to those on the outside everything is said in parables so that,*
>
>> *"'they may be ever seeing but never perceiving,*
>> *and ever hearing but never understanding;*
>> *otherwise they might turn and be forgiven!'"*
>
> (MARK 4:10–12)

That last verse is a problem for many people. What did Jesus mean? Did He speak in parables in order to hide the truth so that people would not understand, so they would not be forgiven? Why would He be so cruel as to hide the truth from people?

It is crucial to understand, however, that this is only one of three explanatory paragraphs Mark provides for us, straight from the lips of Jesus. We cannot take the first paragraph out of context. If we want to understand why Jesus spoke in parables, we must read His explanation in its entirety.

Let's look at the first paragraph, for there Jesus gives us a profound reason for the parables. He points out, first, that there are two kinds of hearers. One class of hearers is the class of Jesus' followers. He says to them, "The secret of the kingdom of God has been given to you." These hearers listen to Jesus and accept His authority as Lord and teacher. To them is given the secret or the mystery of the kingdom of God.

I am fascinated by the secrets and mysteries mentioned in Scripture. Why are they called mysteries? Not because they are vague and difficult to understand. Rather, they are called mysteries because their meaning is not understood by the majority of people. Paul speaks of these same mysteries when he says of himself and his fellow apostles, "So then, men ought to regard us as servants of Christ and as those entrusted with the secret things of God" (1 Corinthians 4:1), the sacred secrets that God has revealed to His followers through the apostles.

What are these mysteries? The inside information on life that only believers are enabled to understand. Mysteries are truths that natural persons cannot discover by themselves. They are the missing pieces of the jigsaw puzzle of life.

Many people from various walks of life stumble on a clue here, a fragment there. Scientists can give us some insights into the nature of life; philosophers can give us other insights; psychologists and psychiatrists can give us a few others; sociologists still others. But the knowledge and insight they provide is always fragmentary and incomplete, and often it is contradictory and misleading. These thinkers and researchers do their best to assemble a complete picture of reality, but their efforts are doomed to failure. Why? Because, as Jesus declares, there are certain missing pieces of the puzzle that only God can supply. And those missing pieces are the most essential pieces of all.

Those missing pieces of the puzzle of life are what Jesus calls "the mysteries of God." The apostle Paul calls them the "deep things of God" (1 Corinthians 2:10) and adds that the natural person cannot understand them, for they are revealed only by the

Spirit of God: "Who among men knows the thoughts of a man except the man's spirit within him? In the same way no one knows the thoughts of God except the Spirit of God" (1 Corinthians 2:11). Only the Spirit of God knows the deep things of God, the enlightening secrets that help you to grasp fully what life is all about. This is not merely theological or mystical mumbo jumbo. This is practical truth for daily living. This truth is hidden from us in our natural state and can be revealed only by God.

The specific mystery Jesus explains to the disciples in this passage is the "secret of the kingdom of God." What does Jesus mean? He refers to an understanding of what God is doing in history—how the events of our day are being used in God's program and planning. The world would have us believe that God is irrelevant to what is going on. If there is a God, then He must have wound up the universe like a clock and walked away. We humans now control world events, and God watches from afar, wringing His hands.

That is not what we learn from God's Word. According to Scripture, God is working out His eternal plan in history, and nothing happens that God does not touch and arrange into a magnificent tapestry of time and space, purpose and meaning. He knows the end from the beginning, and nothing happens anywhere in the universe without His express permission or active instigation. He is the King, and the King is hardly irrelevant to His kingdom. In fact, He is the most relevant and important fact in all the universe.

This is not to say that God overrules our free will, including our freedom to sin. But He is working out a cosmic purpose so vast and sweeping that even our rebellion and disobedience have been accounted for and woven into the eternal design. Even though we have complete moral freedom to do as we wish, God is never surprised by anything we do. That is the mystery of the kingdom of God. And Jesus tells us that the "secret of the kingdom of God has been given to you."

Those on the Outside

Jesus refers to another kind of people as "those on the outside." He says, "But to those on the outside everything is said in parables." Who are these people on the outside? They are all those who are not disciples, not followers of Jesus Christ. Many such people go to church every Sunday, but they are not true disciples of Christ. They do not understand and submit to the lordship of Christ, so the truth is hidden from them. To the people on the outside, the parables are stories without sense, without meaning.

Jesus then said an amazing thing: "But to those on the outside everything is said in parables so that, 'they may be ever seeing but never perceiving, and ever hearing but never understanding; otherwise they might turn and be forgiven!'" This statement troubles many people. It sounds as though Jesus is saying, "There are some people I don't want to repent and receive me as Savior. I don't want them to be my followers, so I've hidden the truth from them to keep them from finding forgiveness." Could Jesus be that cruel and arbitrary? Of course not. That is not His character, so that cannot be what Jesus means.

We will be helped greatly if we understand two things about this account. First, the account is highly condensed. We need the parallel passages in Matthew and Luke to fully understand Jesus' meaning, and we will examine those passages in a moment.

It also helps to understand, as the New International Version shows, that a portion of Jesus' statement is a quotation from the Old Testament. Notice the quotation marks around the words "they may be ever seeing but never perceiving, and ever hearing but never understanding; otherwise they might turn and be forgiven!" Jesus did not originate those words; He is quoting Isaiah 6:9–10. He is saying that this prophecy of Isaiah was being fulfilled in those days, and that fulfillment continues into our time.

Jesus does not say, "I'm speaking in parables so Isaiah's prophecy might be fulfilled." Rather, He is saying, "I'm speaking in parables because Isaiah's prophecy is now being fulfilled." That is a big difference. If you look at Matthew 13:14 you see that this is what has happened. In the parallel passage in Matthew's gospel, the full quotation from Isaiah is given to us: "In them is fulfilled the prophecy of Isaiah: 'You will be ever hearing but never understanding; you will be ever seeing but never perceiving.'" In the original Old Testament passage, Isaiah goes on to explain why this is happening. But Mark leaves this out and quotes only the conclusion. Here is the portion omitted by Mark, as quoted in Matthew 13:15: "'This people's heart has become calloused; they hardly hear with their ears, and they have closed their eyes. Otherwise they might see with their eyes, hear with their ears, understand with their hearts and turn, and I would heal them.'"

The crucial question is who closed their eyes. It was not God. He has not closed His heart against them or refused them forgiveness. The people closed their eyes. It was they who sealed their fate, not God. And why did the people close their eyes? Because they did not want to be healed. That is the point Jesus made. Jesus would have gladly given them healing for their spirits, but they didn't want that. What did they want? Physical healing and nothing more. They wanted Jesus to cure their diseases and restore their physical health so they could go on as before. Knowing this, Jesus said, "You are fulfilling the very words of Isaiah the prophet, in that you are not willing to listen to what I have to say. I came to give you eternal healing, but you want me only to heal your limbs or your skin or your eyes."

Tragically, this is the same attitude with which many people approach the issue of faith healing in our day. They want God to heal their eyesight or their asthma or even their ailing finances, but they aren't interested in the best form of healing, the ultimate and eternal form of healing that Jesus offers. They don't want to be transformed but fixed up and sent on their way. They don't want to be made whole—just happier, healthier, and wealthier.

Jesus saw crowds of such people streaming toward Him, crowding Him, clamoring for Him, pressing against Him. But He knew what was in their hearts. They came for His healing touch but closed their minds when He began to teach. So He spoke to them in parables.

God's Truth: Hidden Like Easter Eggs

The first parable Jesus told was the parable of the sower. We will examine that parable in detail in the next chapter, but we'll now continue to look at His reasons for speaking in parables. Remember, His explanation was divided into three paragraphs, and we have examined only the first one. So let's move to the paragraph beginning with Mark 4:21 and find the second reason Jesus gives for His use of parables.

> He said to them, "Do you bring in a lamp to put it under a bowl or a bed? Instead, don't you put it on its stand? For whatever is hidden is meant to be disclosed, and whatever is concealed is meant to be brought out into the open. If anyone has ears to hear, let him hear."
>
> "Consider carefully what you hear," he continued. "With the measure you use, it will be measured to you—and even more. Whoever has will be given more; whoever does not have, even what he has will be taken from him." (MARK 4:21–25)

In that paragraph are three principles for understanding how parables work. The first is given in verses 21–22: "Do you bring in a lamp to put it under a bowl or a bed?" Of course not! "Instead, don't you put it on its stand?" Absolutely! The purpose of light is to illuminate and reveal; it makes no sense to conceal a light source. Jesus is talking about why He speaks in parables, and in the process He is about to reveal a paradox. He says, "Whatever is hidden is meant to be disclosed, and whatever is concealed is meant to be brought out into the open."

To put it plainly, Jesus says that hiding the truth makes truth more visible. Isn't that an amazing statement? That is the paradox. And what is a paradox? It is a statement that seems contradictory or opposed to common sense and yet is true. It is a deep truth wrapped within an enigma. And the paradox Jesus presents to us is this: if you hide the truth slightly, the truth becomes easier to see.

Every morning when I get up I stand in front of a mirror, not to admire what I see, which is discouraging, but in order to shave. My mirror has two lights, one on either side, capable of yielding two different intensities of light, bright and dim. I have learned that if I turn the lights on bright, the intense glare makes it hard to see my face in the mirror. The only way I can shave success-fully is to dim the lights; then I can see what I am doing. When the light is dimmer, my face is easier to see.

In a similar way, the direct teaching of Jesus was so brilliant in its intensity and power that many of the people could not absorb it directly. But by muting the glare of His message by wrapping it in stories, Jesus enabled His listeners—those with receptive hearts—to better understand His meaning. You find this same principle in Proverbs 25:2: "It is the glory of God to conceal a matter; to search out a matter is the glory of kings."

God loves to conceal truth. Oh, the truth can be found. God doesn't conceal it behind concrete barriers but behind gauzy, silken layers of intrigue, mystery, and fascination. That is why His mysteries are so enjoyable to unravel. We are all intrigued by mystery, by things cryptic and hidden. We love to search them out. God appeals to this side of human nature and hides His truth from us in places where it can be found only with care and effort. But the beautiful paradox of God's truth is that He hides it only to make it more visible. He does this in the spiritual realm. And He does this in nature.

How much truth God has hidden away in the world of nature all around us! Through the centuries, scientists and philosophers have puzzled over the nature of reality, trying to work out such mysteries as the meaning of time, the nature of gravity, the structure of the atom, the properties of light, the secrets of DNA and the genetic code. As human thinkers have delved into the deep nature of physical reality, they have discovered the answer to one secret only to reveal ten or a hundred more mysteries to draw them on. One truth leads to another, with each new discovery changing the course of human life and human history. These truths have been concealed within the fabric of the universe so that human beings might find them.

God's concealment of truth is reminiscent of parents concealing Easter eggs for their children to find on Easter morning. Parents usually hide the eggs just well enough to make the hunt fun and interesting but always leaving them visible enough to be found. Understanding this principle, Jesus knew that people would grasp the truth more readily if He cloaked it in a parable.

In Mark 4:24, Jesus reveals another principle. "Consider carefully what you hear," He says. "With the measure you use, it will be measured to you—and even more." In other words, if you search for truth, you will discover far more than you ever expected to find. You cannot find truth unless you seek truth, but if you seek God's truth, particularly the truth of His Word, you will find more than you ever dreamed possible. So seek His truth. Search the Scriptures, ask and pray, study and devour His principles for your life. Then God's truth will flow into your life like a stream or even a flood of life-giving water.

We find another key principle in Mark 4:25, where we read, "Whoever has will be given more; whoever does not have, even what he has will be taken from him." "But that's not fair!" you may say. Perhaps it is not, but it's true nonetheless. That's the way life is. It's a basic rule of life: if you do not use what you have, you lose it. Anyone who has ever had an arm in a sling knows that it takes time, after the cast and sling are removed, to regain use of the arm. If you learn calculus or French or some other subject in high school but don't use that knowledge for years afterwards, you lose it. You remember fragments and snatches, but you would flunk a test that you could have easily passed when you were in school. The same is true in our spiritual lives. We have been given so many opportunities and blessings, but if we do not seize the opportunities and apply those blessings to our lives, we will surely lose them.

Use it or lose it is a principle of life. And God does not want us to lose the benefit of the truth that He has disclosed to us. That is why Jesus spoke in parables. These principles are true and practical, and He wants us to apply them and hold onto them for life.

Able to Bear the Truth

Mark next records two more parables of Jesus, the parable of the secretly growing grain and the parable of the mustard seed. We will pass over these for now but will examine them in depth in the next chapters. Moving on, we see the Lord as He concludes His explanation for speaking in parables.

> *With many similar parables Jesus spoke the word to them, as much as they could understand. He did not say anything to them without using a parable. But when he was alone with his own disciples, he explained everything.*
> (MARK 4:33–34)

Again we see a reference to two classes of hearers. Jesus preached to everyone in parables; in fact, He didn't preach anything from then on without using parables. But when He was alone with the disciples, He disclosed the hidden truths of the parables.

Here we also see an important rule about revelation. Jesus gave to the people, Mark says, as much truth as they could understand. On another occasion, Jesus told His disciples, "I have much more to say to you, more than you can now bear" (John 16:12). Jesus teaches us only what we can bear, only what we can receive and incorporate into our lives. He doesn't throw all truth at us at once. That would destroy us.

The glory and wonder of the Scriptures is that they are put together in such a way that it takes the Word and the Spirit to understand the Bible. You can read the Word, but if your heart is not prepared by the Spirit, the words will mean nothing to you. If you are open to what the Spirit is saying to you, the Scriptures will make sense and change your mind and heart. The beautiful thing about the Scripture is that there is so much truth and meaning embedded in its words that you can return to them again and again. Each time you read, you will discover some new truth you never saw before.

Why doesn't God give us all of the layers of truth that are embedded in His Word once and for all? Because we could not bear it. Each time we read a Bible passage, He opens our eyes to the truth we are able to bear at that moment.

But it is not only God's revelation of Himself that must be given to us a little at a time, as we are able to bear it. He also reveals the truth about ourselves in the same way. He shows us ourselves a little at a time, because He is so loving and gracious. Why? Because we can bear to see the truth about ourselves only a little at a time. God does not rip the veil off and expose the whole ghastly truth about ourselves all at once. If He did, we would be destroyed by the truth.

God gently lifts the veil and lets us see ourselves an inch at a time, letting us get used to each new and terrible revelation before He shows us the next. With each little revelation, we shake and weep and moan, "Is that the real me? Please, don't show me any more!" We see how we have hurt others with our words, or how we have set a bad example for our children, or how we have engaged in some shameful sin. And we are aghast! When we think we've gotten to the bottom of it, God lifts the veil a little more, and we are devastated again. But as God reveals our sin and failure to us, He also reveals His forgiveness, grace, and adequacy to handle it. He gives us as much as we can bear, no more.

This is why it takes a lifetime to understand the Scriptures. This is why you can spend your life studying God's Word and never feel you have mastered it. God's truth is so deep and wide, so rich and vast, that we cannot bear it all at once. Jesus understood our limitations, and so He tailored His message to fit within the limits of our understanding. He gave us the light of His revelation but dimmed its brilliance so that we would not be dazzled or blinded but enlightened.

eight

Seeds of Truth

➤ **Mark 4:3–9, 13–20, 26–32**

Herman Melville, the author of *Moby Dick*, was not only a great writer but also a great oral storyteller. One evening, Melville was visiting at the Massachusetts home of his friend and fellow novelist, Nathaniel Hawthorne. During the evening, Melville related to Hawthorne and his wife a number of adventures he had during a voyage in the South Seas. He described one particularly gruesome battle he had witnessed between two island warrior tribes. The Hawthornes were engrossed in Melville's tale, which was accompanied by vivid descriptions and exuberant gestures.

A few days later, Hawthorne stopped by Melville's house and said, "Could you bring out that club? I'd like to see it again."

"Club?" said Melville, bewildered. "What club?"

"The one you were swinging about your head while you told us about the island battle."

"But I had no club," said Melville, his bewilderment deepening.

"Of course you did," insisted Hawthorne. "I distinctly recall it. So does my wife. You brought that club back from the South Seas. It was black and carved and . . . "

"But I tell you," said Melville, "I had no club!"

In the end, it became clear what had happened. Melville's storytelling had been so vivid, so exciting, so captivating that Mr. and Mrs. Hawthorne became convinced they had seen their friend swinging a club around him as he told his story. Such is the power of a well-told story.

Seated at the Feet of the Master

In the previous chapter, we looked at Jesus' purpose in teaching through parables, as that purpose is explained for us in Mark 4. Now we return to Mark 4 and look at the parables themselves, at what they mean and how we can apply their truth to our lives.

We will seat ourselves among the disciples, sitting on the grass at the Master's feet, listening as He explains the mysteries of the kingdom of God—vital truths about humanity and reality that cannot be found in psychology, sociology, physics, or other secular studies. Yet these are essential truths that we must know about ourselves and the world in which we live in order to fulfill our human purpose.

Mark relates only three parables from our Lord's first day of teaching in parables, but he adds, "With many similar parables Jesus spoke the word to them" (Mark 4:33). Matthew records seven parables given on this occasion. The three that Mark selects are the parable of the sower, the parable of the secretly growing grain, and the parable of the mustard seed. Each is a revelation of the invisible reign of God in human affairs. Jesus takes us behind the scenes in each of these parables and shows us something about the way God acts in human life. In the process, He reveals to us the mysteries of the kingdom of God.

The point of each parable emerges clearly as we understand what Jesus has explained to us. The first, the parable of the sower, is intended to show us how the kingdom comes into a human life, how our eyes are opened, and what God is doing. The second, the parable of the secretly growing grain, shows us how the kingdom grows and how our knowledge of ourselves and God increases. The last, the parable of the mustard seed, shows us a surprising effect the kingdom will have in the world.

That is the outline we will follow in this study of the three parables. Now let's look at each of these parables in turn, beginning with the parable of the sower.

> *"Listen! A farmer went out to sow his seed. As he was scattering the seed, some fell along the path, and the birds came and ate it up. Some fell on rocky places, where it did not have much soil. It sprang up quickly, because the soil was shallow. But when the sun came up, the plants were scorched, and they withered because they had no root. Other seed fell among thorns, which grew up and choked the plants, so that they did not bear grain. Still other seed fell on good soil. It came up, grew and produced a crop, multiplying thirty, sixty, or even a hundred times."*
>
> *Then Jesus said, "He who has ears to hear, let him hear."*
> (MARK 4:3–9)

This was the first of Jesus' parables. It is typical of the way He liked to illustrate spiritual truths from nature. I think it is probable that He selected an example that the people could look around and see for themselves. Jesus stood by the lake, and the crowd was spread across the hillside. Perhaps the people could look out along the road by the lakeshore and see a field where a man was sowing grain. Perhaps Jesus plucked an example from that moment, taking the sower's activity as His text, and told the story as the crowd watched it happening before their eyes. They could see the seed falling on various kinds of soil. They could see the birds landing and eating some of the seed. They could feel the heat of the sun beating on their necks. I believe that everything Jesus told the people was being dramatically enacted before their eyes.

When Jesus said, "He who has ears to hear, let him hear," He made it evident that this is much more than just a story. It was not meant merely to entertain. Jesus was urging the people to think about what He was telling them. Even so, they did not understand. Afterwards, the Twelve gathered around Him and said, "Explain the parable to us." So Jesus said, "The secret of the kingdom of God has been given to you." And as He explained, He said something truly significant for us.

> *Jesus said to them, "Don't you understand this parable?*
> *How then will you understand any parable?"* (MARK 4:13)

This is a crucial statement. Jesus is telling us that the parable of the sower is the key to interpreting all the parables. If we do not grasp the meaning of this parable, the words of all the other parables will be unintelligible. If we do not use this first parable as the lens for examining all the others, we will make the same mistake made by many Bible commentators who make these parables mean whatever they want them to mean.

The Rosetta Stone of Parables

A brief story from history provides an analogy of the importance of the parable of the sower.

In 1799, a French soldier was walking in the Nile Delta region of Egypt, near the town of Rashid (Rosetta). Napoleon had recently conquered the area and constructed a fort where the soldier was stationed. As he walked near the fort, the soldier stubbed his foot against a slab of black basalt. Bending closer and brushing away the sand, the soldier saw that the slab was covered with carved inscriptions in three languages—Egyptian hiero-glyphs at the top, then an Egyptian cursive script called Demotic, and at the bottom, Greek.

Inspection revealed that the Greek and Demotic inscriptions were translations of the Egyptian hieroglyphs. The hieroglyphs had been carved in 196 B.C. in honor of the Egyptian king Ptolemy V. The stone was a truly amazing find, because all knowl-edge of how to read hieroglyphs had been lost for more than fourteen hundred years, and this stone became known as the Rosetta Stone. With its discovery, thousands of once-mysterious symbols on ancient palace walls, in desert tombs, and on dry, cracking papyrus fragments suddenly became meaningful and alive. Scores of ancient secrets were revealed. One inscription on a single black stone proved to be the key to understanding every other inscription of an ancient empire.

In a similar way, this one parable, the parable of the sower, provides the key to understanding every other parable of the kingdom of God. The parable of the sower is the Rosetta Stone of all parables. We do not have to scratch our heads and wonder what the parables mean. The rules for understanding the parables have been given to us in the parable of the sower.

Unfortunately some Bible commentators choose to make up rules of interpretation as they go along. A typical example of this misguided school of thought is the following statement by a scholar who has been widely read among evangelical Christians:

> The parables must never be treated as allegories. In an allegory, every part and action and detail of the story has an inner meaning and significance. *Pilgrim's Progress*

and *The Faerie Queen* are allegories. In them, every event and person and detail has a symbolic meaning. But, if that be so, clearly an allegory is something to be read and studied and examined and investigated. But a parable is something which was heard once, and once only.

This scholar suggests that we need not probe into the details of the parables. We need only get one general point and move on. But Jesus tells us, "He who has ears to hear, let him hear"—a strong invitation to examine, investigate, and give close study. Now listen to the way Jesus interprets the parable of the sower.

> *Then Jesus said to them, "Don't you understand this parable? How then will you understand any parable? The farmer sows the word. Some people are like seed along the path, where the word is sown. As soon as they hear it, Satan comes and takes away the word that was sown in them. Others, like seed sown on rocky places, hear the word and at once receive it with joy. But since they have no root, they last only a short time. When trouble or persecution comes because of the word, they quickly fall away. Still others, like seed sown among thorns, hear the word; but the worries of this life, the deceitfulness of wealth and the desires for other things come in and choke the word, making it unfruitful. Others, like seed sown on good soil, hear the word, accept it, and produce a crop—thirty, sixty or even a hundred times what was sown."* (MARK 4:13–20)

Notice that Jesus treats His parable exactly as the commentator says we must not do. He treats it as an allegory. Our Lord says that every detail means something. Furthermore, He tells us that this is the way to interpret all the parables. This is the key to understanding parables. Parables are allegories in which every detail is important and has application.

The Sower and the Four Soils

Let's look at the parable of the sower and see the first of these secrets of the kingdom: the secret of how the kingdom of God comes to us.

Jesus tells us that the sower goes out and sows, and the Word is what he sows. That is how the kingdom arrives in human hearts. The Word of God is sown by means of preaching, teaching, witnessing, or even the writing of books such as this one. The Word is dropped into human hearts like seeds scattered into the soil. That Word is the life-giving element that can bring enrichment and harvest into a human life. So the moment of the sowing of the Word is a magical hour. It is a time of opportunity—the opportunity for a human life to be transformed.

I used to read this story as though the various soils represented four different kinds of people, four static personalities who remained the same through their lifetimes. Some were permanently hard-hearted, some were impulsive, some were full of concerns, and so forth. But I have come to see that what our Lord describes is not permanent personality types but conditions of the heart at the given moment when the Word is being sown. I don't know of anyone who exists in one unchanging condition throughout life. We go through cycles and phases. Whenever the Word is being sown in our lives, we are in one or another of the cycles or phases that Jesus describes. We have all been callous at times, when we have heard the Word; at other times we have been impulsive and emotionally shallow; at still other times we have been overly concerned about mundane matters. And by the grace

of God, we have all experienced times of being open and responsive to the Word.

What is your heart like now? You are in one of these four
conditions. Which one? That is a question only you can answer.
Let's look at each of these four conditions in turn.

First, there is the hardened, callous heart. The seed is sown
on the beaten, trodden-down pathway as hard and impenetrable
as asphalt. This represents people whose hearts are closed
because their lives are full of busyness, cynicism, and self-
centeredness. When the seed hits such a hardened heart, the
birds come and gather it up immediately. In other words, the
seed of God's Word is snatched away by Satan before it has even
a few moments to take root in a person's life.

C. S. Lewis, in the opening chapter of *The Screwtape Letters,*
describes a man who goes into a library to read and meditate. His
mind is suddenly opened to deep thoughts of God. Confronted
with his standing before God, he starts thinking in terms of his
eternal welfare. But, Lewis says, there are demons assigned to this
fellow. It is their unholy task to keep him from discovering God's
truth. So they call attention to the fact that it is lunchtime, and he
is hungry. The man figures he will go get a bite to eat, then return
and resume his study of God's truth. But as he leaves the library
and steps out onto the street, the demon calls his attention to the
street noises—a passing bus, a newsboy calling out the latest head-
lines, and so forth. These distractions are all it takes. All thoughts
of God disappear from the man's mind, and he returns to his old,
mundane worldview. That is an accurate but disturbing description of what happens to the callous human mind and heart.

The second condition Jesus describes is that of the impulsive
heart. The seed falls on the heart of such a person, and he or she
immediately responds with joy. The seed takes root and grows up

quickly. The trouble is, such people respond like this to the latest spiritual fad, food fad, book fad, political fad, movie fad, whatever the new thing may be. We all can get caught up in this kind of thinking at one time or another. If we are in such a condition when God's Word comes to us, our lives are so shallow that the Word cannot take deep root and truly change us. We might give the temporary appearance of a changed life, but the transformation was skin-deep at best. God's truth cannot take root in such a life but withers away and dies. Jesus says that this kind of life is shallow; it cannot stand the heat. When persecution and tribulation come, it dries up and blows away.

The third condition Jesus describes is that of the overinvolved heart. This condition is represented by the thorns. There are people who hear the Word, but thorns spring up and choke it. What kinds of thorns was Jesus talking about?

There are, first, cares and worries. Some people are continually fretting about what is going to happen next. They are anxious and cannot leave control of their lives in God's hands. When the seed of the Word falls on their hearts, they are too bound up by anxiety and worry to receive it.

Then there are people who delight in riches. They are caught up in the pursuit of wealth, pleasure, and status. That is all that their lives consist of. The life-giving Word, which could make real men and women out of them, cannot find root and grow. A heart full of greed and pleasure seeking has no room for God.

There is also what Jesus calls "the desires for other things," or what we might call restlessness. These people are never content but always seeking some new experience, some new emotional high, some new relationship, some new way of thinking about reality. They are spiritual and emotional drifters and vagabonds. The Word cannot take root in their lives, because they cannot make a commitment to it. They have to be moving on. So the Word is choked out of their lives.

The final condition Jesus describes is the beautiful condition of the receptive heart. This is the open, ready, responsive heart, the heart that gladly receives the seed of God's Word and allows it to put down deep, healthy roots.

I once had a conversation with a prominent businessman who explained to me how he became a Christian. He had been reared without any church background or Christian instruction. He had four different sets of foster parents before he was eighteen. Growing up, he had tried various philosophies, including Eastern religion, seeking some answers to the riddle of life. One day a friend invited him to church, and he went for the first time in his life. The pastor spoke about how to have a relationship with Jesus Christ.

Afterward, the man met the pastor and said, "Sir, if I understand you correctly, Christianity says that God is up there and man is down here. Between them is Jesus Christ, and He is the only way for man to bridge the gap between himself and God. Is that right?"

The pastor said, "That's exactly right. In fact, you've just described a verse in Scripture that says, 'For there is one God and one mediator between God and men, the man Christ Jesus'" (1 Timothy 2:5).

"Well," the businessman replied, "that makes sense to me."

"I have a book I'd like to give you," said the pastor. "If you would, I'd like you to read it, then come back next week and we'll talk about it together."

The man accepted the book, then said, "But tell me: If it is true that Jesus is the way to God, why do I have to wait until next week? Why can't I come to Him now? If it really works, it will work now; if it doesn't work, it never will."

The pastor agreed. So they bowed their heads, and the man received Jesus Christ as his Lord and Savior. He received the Word and has grown in grace and Christian maturity ever since. He has become an effective witness for Christ, and other people have been brought to the Lord by his testimony.

That is a responsive heart! It is a heart that is ready to act. Whenever the Word falls on human hearts, the seed is being sown. Individual hearts are either ready to respond, as this man was, or the seed will be stolen away, choked out, or withered before it can take hold. That is the way the kingdom of God comes into our hearts. The great question, then, is this: As you examine the state of your life and soul, what is the condition of your heart? Is it receptive and responsive, or is it hard, barren, or thorn-infested?

Only you know the answer to that question.

The Parable of the Secretly Growing Grain

In His second parable in Mark 4, our Lord speaks of the seed that grows in secret.

> *He also said, "This is what the kingdom of God is like. A man scatters seed on the ground. Night and day, whether he sleeps or gets up, the seed sprouts and grows, though he does not know how. All by itself the soil produces grain— first the stalk, then the head, then the full kernel in the head. As soon as the grain is ripe, he puts the sickle to it, because the harvest has come."* (MARK 4:26–29)

This is a secret of the kingdom of God. And I find this one of the most encouraging of all the parables Jesus ever told. He is speaking of how the rule of God increases and grows in our lives.

If we patiently expect God to work, Jesus tells us, then we will surely see His harvest in our lives. The key to this whole passage is that "the seed sprouts and grows, though he does not know how. All by itself the soil produces grain." In other words, there are forces at work that will faithfully perform their work. We do not know how these forces work, and we do not need to know. Those forces will bring about the harvest, even though we do not understand the workings of those forces. We cannot hurry the harvest by fretting and worrying. We must let God work, and He will work. We can rest secure and confident in that assurance.

In this word picture, a farmer goes out to sow seed in a grain field. It is hard work, but once he has sown the seed, he has done what he can do. At the end of the workday, he goes home and goes to bed. He does not sit up all night biting his fingernails, wondering if the seed fell in the right places so that it will take root. Nor does he rise the next morning and dig up the seed to see if it has sprouted yet. He rests secure in the fact that God is at work. Yes, he has a part in this process, and he must do his part; no one else can do his job for him. But having faithfully performed his function, he rests secure, knowing that as the seed grows, it will follow predictable, observable stages: "first the stalk, then the head, then the full kernel in the head." Only when the grain is ready for harvest is it time for him to act once more.

This is the same principle Paul describes for us in his first letter to the Corinthians:

> *I planted the seed, Apollos watered it, but God made it grow. So neither he who plants nor he who waters is anything, but only God, who makes things grow. The man who plants and the man who waters have one purpose, and each*

will be rewarded according to his own labor. For we are God's fellow workers. (1 CORINTHIANS 3:6–9)

This is how we should expect God to work. The seed of the Word is spread by the witness of Christians, perhaps with a word of teaching or exhortation. Over time, a quiet yet relentless process takes place, requiring time and patience on our part as we allow God to work. Unfortunately many of us lack the patience that is required. Some people demand instant results, and that spirit of impatience is one of the most destructive forces at work in the church. We want immediate conversions, immediate responses every time the Word is preached. We fail to allow sufficient time—God's time—for the Word to take root, grow, and come to harvest. If we want to see God's harvest, we must learn patience.

There is a young man whose life I observed over a period of years. He and his family became a part of our congregation when he was in elementary school. As he entered adolescence, he went through a time of deep and bitter rebellion against God. I saw his parents in tears, hurt and crushed by his defiance and rejection of their faith. Yet they never ceased to pray for him, talk to him, and show love for him.

Throughout that tumultuous and tortuous process, a seed was sown in that boy's heart that slowly took root and began to grow. When I say "slowly," I mean the change in his attitudes was almost imperceptible. Yet, if you looked closely, amid his youthful rage and insolence, you could occasionally catch a faint hint of softening, of relenting, of repenting. In time, he returned to the Lord and opened up to his Christian parents. Within a few years, he was in seminary, training to become a pastor.

That is how the Word often grows in a human heart—slowly, gradually, secretly. The sower of the Word does not know how it happens, nor can he take any credit for the results. But he can rest secure in the knowledge that God is at work. Although we have our little part to play, the results do not depend on us. Everything depends on Him.

The Puzzling Parable of the Mustard Seed

The parable of the mustard seed is the last of this trilogy of parables. Mark records:

> Again he said, "What shall we say the kingdom of God is like, or what parable shall we use to describe it? It is like a mustard seed, which is the smallest seed you plant in the ground. Yet when planted, it grows and becomes the largest of all garden plants, with such big branches that the birds of the air can perch in its shade." (MARK 4:30–32)

This is one of the most puzzling of Jesus' parables. Many Bible scholars pondered this parable without conclusion, because it seems contrary to nature. Mustard seeds do not grow into great shrubs with large branches in which birds build nests. There are trees called mustard trees, but they are not true mustard plants. What, then, is Jesus talking about?

I think we get a clue to the strange character of this parable in the way our Lord introduces it: "What shall we say the kingdom of God is like, or what parable shall we use to describe it?" He sounds almost puzzled, as if He is asking, "Hmm, how can I illustrate this? With what can I compare the kingdom of God?" There is an elusive aspect of the kingdom of God, so elusive that even Jesus is hard-pressed to find a natural illustration for it.

Then His thinking settles on a suitable parable: the parable of the mustard seed.

Anyone who is familiar with the New Testament is aware that Jesus frequently used the mustard seed as a symbol of faith. In Matthew 17:20, for example, He says, "I tell you the truth, if you have faith as small as a mustard seed, you can say to this mountain, 'Move from here to there' and it will move." We in Christian circles have picked up the metaphor of the mustard seed, and we often use it as a symbol of faith. Why is the mustard seed such an apt metaphor to suggest what faith is all about? Because this seed has two crucial faithlike qualities.

First, the mustard seed is a tiny seed with an astounding capacity for growth. Like faith, a mustard seed starts small and rapidly expands. But just as an unplanted, unwatered seed cannot grow, so an unused, untried faith cannot grow. But faith, when used, always increases. That is why you never have to worry about whether your faith is small or great. If it is small, it can grow with use and become large. Trust God in the little things, and you will gain the faith to step out and take on the great things. That is an invariable principle of the Word of God.

Second, the mustard seed is pungent. It stimulates and irritates. Take a spoonful of real, full-strength mustard, the potent, pale yellow mustard you find in Chinese restaurants. Just one teaspoon of hot Chinese mustard, made from pure ground mustard seed, will make you feel as though the top of your head will pop off. The pungency of the mustard seed comes from a powerful enzyme called myrosin. That powerful, irritating enzyme is the reason mustard has been used for more than three thousand years as a condiment and a medicine.

When I was a boy in Montana, we had no doctors or medicines. Instead, we relied on home remedies when we caught a bad cold. A typical home remedy was a mustard plaster, a sticky, smelly, gooey mess concocted of flour, dry mustard powder, and scalding water or milk. Applied steaming hot to the victim (and yes, *victim* is the appropriate word!), it quickly begins to irritate and burn the skin. It also stimulates the flesh to turn red. If you leave it on too long the skin will blister. I don't understand how a mustard plaster works, but it seemed to cure the common cold in those days. (At the very least, it made me reluctant to admit I had one.)

That is what mustard does. It irritates and stimulates. And it is important to note, so does faith. If your faith is growing, then you will be stimulating the faith of others around you to grow. Soon that stimulus spreads throughout the Christian body, and people will begin to walk in faith in new, bold ways. The same faith that stimulates fellow Christians to growth will also irritate the non-Christian world, leading to persecution and backlash. If you are being persecuted for your faith, then it is likely that your faith is just as Jesus described it: mustardlike and irritating to the people who have no faith. That is to be expected, said Jesus, because that is what the kingdom of God is like.

True Mustard and False Growth

The startling thing about this parable is that the mustard seed Jesus describes does not behave like true mustard seeds in nature. No other mustard seed has ever grown as did the mustard seed in this parable. True mustard plants are shrubs that rarely grow taller than five or six feet. In fact, the small stature of the mustard plant and the pungent flavor of its seed suggest to my mind what the church ought to be—lowly and unimpressive, but with a powerful, even pungent, influence on society. Mustard plants are spindly, fragile shrubs with dense yellow flowers. They do not grow branches capable of supporting a nest of birds, as Jesus proclaims in His parable.

Why, then, does Jesus picture the mustard plant as a great, impressive treelike plant, probably twenty feet high, with large branches capable of supporting the birds and their nests? True mustard has never grown like that anywhere in the world. What Jesus suggests is contrary to the nature of mustard seeds, and the people hearing His parable surely knew that.

Yet I believe Jesus gave an example that doesn't occur in nature for a reason: He was revealing to us a secret of the kingdom of God.

Jesus says that this mustard seed, which is supposed to be lowly and unimpressive, will provoke a false growth. It will stimulate a false system that will be characterized by an ambition to be dominant, impressive, and powerful. It will seek worldwide influence, and as a result, satanic forces will take up residence in its vast structure. Those satanic forces are represented by the birds that nest in the branches of the mustard plant.

How do we know that the birds represent evil? Remember that the parable of the sower is the key, the Rosetta Stone, to all the other parables of our Lord. Jesus taught us that every element in a parable has a symbolic meaning, and the birds in the parable of the sower represented satanic forces that snatch the Word of God away from human hearts. When we come to the parable of the mustard seed, we find the symbol of the birds once more. So, using the parable of the sower as our Rosetta Stone, it becomes obvious what the birds nesting in the mustard plant represent: evil forces, satanic forces, that invade and nest within the kingdom.

Remember that Jesus has painted a word picture of a false and unnatural mustard plant. True, the mustard plant begins from the genuine mustard seed of faith, but a false and strange growth soon takes over. The Lord's hearers knew that He was describing a kind of fantastic, unbelievable mustard plant the like of which they had never seen before. No doubt they were perplexed and confused by what He was describing, for the truth is, Jesus was speaking prophetically about something that would not come to pass in the lifetime of those who first heard the parable.

In the parable of the mustard seed, Jesus described an approaching kingdom that would be tremendously powerful and would be called the kingdom of God. Yet it would be anything but. After twenty centuries of Christian history, we can see what Jesus was talking about. Great church institutions have grown up, seeking worldly power and influence, seeking to dominate political life and influence people through worldly power. You may think, *Oh, he's describing the Roman Catholic Church, with its past history of politically corrupt popes, the sale of indulgences, the terror of the Inquisition, and so forth.* That's true, but I am also describing many Protestant churches, including some that are thought of as evangelical. I believe Jesus is talking about any church that portrays itself as being a branch of the true kingdom of God but that operates by the power structures and systems of this fallen world.

I am always amazed at the things evangelicals regard as marks of a successful church. Usually people think that the sign of spiritual success is big numbers: the bigger the crowd, the more successful the church. But the truth is that it's easy to attract big crowds. All you have to do is preach a message people want to hear, a message that dilutes biblical truth, a message that makes God a genie in a bottle instead of our Lord and Master. The cults attract huge crowds by compromising biblical truth. We should not be so impressed by large numbers, for by God's standards, numbers are never a sign of true success.

We are also impressed by churches with big budgets, impressive structures, costly art and architecture. But these are not the signs of true success either. We should remember the warning of Jesus to churches that aspire to wealth: "You say, 'I am rich; I have acquired wealth and do not need a thing.' But you do not realize that you are wretched, pitiful, poor, blind and naked" (Revelation 3:17). Jesus then urges the church to buy from Him true riches, "gold refined in the fire," which is genuine faith and spiritual maturity that can come only through the refining fire of testing and obedience. But wealth is not in any way a mark of success in the true church of Jesus Christ.

So what is the mark of success? The apostle Paul called on the church in Ephesus to "live a life worthy of the calling you have received" (Ephesians 4:1). Worthy living, Paul explained, is characterized by certain qualities and actions: "Be completely humble and gentle; be patient, bearing with one another in love. Make every effort to keep the unity of the Spirit through the bond of peace" (Ephesians 4:2–3). That is a successful church, a church where people are growing in humility, gentleness, patience, love, unity, and peace.

Three Parables and Three Secrets Revealed

In Mark 4, we have seen three secrets of the kingdom of God revealed through the parables of Jesus. What do these parables say to us? They tell us that God is at work today just as He was then.

First, God sows His Word by various means in our lives and hearts. The condition of our hearts, at the moment His Word is given to us, determines whether we are ready and responsive or closed and unreceptive. We must take care that our hearts are always ready and open to receive His Word.

Second, we are to rest on Him. The battle is the Lord's, not ours. He is working out His purposes in our individual lives, in the life of His church, and throughout His world. We have our little part to play, but He is the Lord of the harvest. He will accomplish His will in the world. We can rest until the harvest comes, and then He will call us to action again.

Third and finally, as followers of Jesus Christ and members of His church, we are to be humble and loving, not seeking status or advancement but stimulating one another to greater faith, in the same way a mustard seed stimulates. As we live out our faith, we can be sure that we will be provoking a false system, a false kingdom resembling the kingdom of God in form but false and deceptive in its substance. It will rise around us on all sides, and evil will nest in its branches. Even so, we must be true to Christ and to our faith. We must walk worthy of God, living as He has called us to live.

With these truths, Jesus began to teach the people in parables. And there is much more that He taught them, with His astounding words and His amazing deeds.

nine

Why Are You Afraid?

➤ **Mark 4:35–5:20**

Army Corporal Jacob DeShazer had been reared by Christian parents but had never received Jesus Christ as Lord and Savior. On April 18, 1942, he climbed into a B-25 bomber and took off from the deck of the aircraft carrier *Hornet*. DeShazer was the bombardier on a one-way mission commanded by Lieutenant Colonel Jimmy Doolittle, part of a force of sixteen planes and seventy-nine men. They did not have enough fuel for a round trip, so their mission was to drop their bombs, then proceed to Japanese-held China and either bail out or crash land. Knowing they would almost certainly be killed or captured, they volunteered for a chance to deliver a demoralizing blow to the Imperial Japanese forces and a big morale boost for the Allies.

As Jacob DeShazer's plane came in low over the land, he looked out the nose of the plane and saw Japanese people looking up at him, smiling and waving. They thought the bomber was one of their own. Up ahead was the target: a group of massive oil storage tanks. DeShazer checked his bomb sights and dropped his ordnance on cue. Incendiary bombs exploded, enveloping the target in billowing flames. Flak bursts punched several holes in the plane as it fled east toward China.

Hours later, as the plane was running out of fuel, DeShazer and his fellow airmen prepared to jump. As he looked out the open door at the inky night sky, Jacob DeShazer knew fear and contemplated death. When he was young and life was simple, DeShazer had seen no reason to pray for help from God. Now, as his chances for survival hovered somewhere between slim and none, he couldn't bring himself to pray. He hadn't prayed in years and saw no reason to start praying now. So, as he jumped out of the doomed B-25, the leap he took was not a leap of faith. It was a fearful leap into the dark unknown.

What DeShazer didn't know but would later learn was that his mother was praying for him at that exact moment. Although she didn't know where he was or what he was doing, she was praying for his safety and for his soul.

DeShazer came to earth in a Chinese graveyard. The landing broke several of his ribs. Within hours, he was captured by Japanese soldiers and taken to a prison for interrogation. Brought before a high official of the Japanese occupation, he was sentenced to death. "At sunrise," the official told him, "I shall personally have the honor of cutting off your head." DeShazer didn't sleep that night; the fear and horror of death by decapitation was all he could think about. The next morning, he was blindfolded and led from his cell. The blindfold was removed, and there was a blinding flash, but it turned out to be a camera flash. There was no execution; the official had lied.

DeShazer and his fellow prisoners were taken to Tokyo to be interrogated and tortured. Torture consisted of being hung by the hands from pegs, being strapped to a chair and beaten, and being nearly drowned. After that, he was sent back to China and spent two years in a narrow, darkened cell. In that cell, summers were boiling hot, and winters were unbearably cold. He endured dysentery and other illnesses, as well as the brutality of the guards.

In 1944, after two years in captivity, DeShazer was allowed to have something to read—a Bible. He could have it for three weeks and than would have to pass it on to the next prisoner. DeShazer read by the light of a tiny, slitlike window near the top of his cell. He began in Genesis and read straight through Revelation. And the words of that Book came to life in his hands. He was particularly struck by what he read in the Old Testament. From boyhood, he had heard about the life of Christ. But he was astonished to find that the prophecies of the Old Testament, written centuries before Jesus was born, depicted His life and ministry with nearly as much detail and clarity as the gospels themselves.

DeShazer memorized as much of the Bible as he could. He remembered how his mother had invited him many times to receive Jesus as his Lord and Savior. The gospel had never made sense to him before. Now it was the only thing in this crazy world that did make sense. On June 8, 1944, he made Jesus the Lord of his life, and that decision put an end to the fear that had been a constant enemy after his capture.

One day, soon after his conversion, a sadistic guard slammed the cell door on DeShazer's foot and stomped on it. At first, as he cradled his throbbing foot, DeShazer could think of nothing but hatred for the guard. But he remembered Jesus' words: "Love your enemies and pray for those who persecute you" (Matthew 5:44). The next day, DeShazer greeted the guard with a word of blessing in Japanese and asked about the guard's family. DeShazer continued to show kindness to the guard day after day, and the man responded by treating DeShazer kindly, bringing him extra food and even candy.

On August 6, 1945, Jacob DeShazer awoke at 7 A.M., sensing an urging from the Lord that he should pray for an end to the war. He got up and prayed intensely for seven hours straight. Finally, at 2 P.M., DeShazer felt a sense of peace wash over him, as if the Spirit of God were saying, "Everything is all right now. The victory is won." A few days later, he learned that even as he was praying for peace, an atomic bomb had exploded over Hiroshima, Japan. The war was over.

During his imprisonment, Jacob DeShazer developed a deep compassion and concern for the Japanese people, and he felt God calling him to return to Japan as a missionary. He and his wife, Florence, fulfilled that calling from 1948 until their retirement in 1978. They planted many churches and led many Japanese people to Christ. One of those who was led to Christ by his testimony was Mitsuo Fuchida, the flight commander who led the Japanese attack on Pearl Harbor. Fuchida later became an international evangelist.

That is the power of God to replace fear with faith, hate with compassion, a thirst for revenge with a hunger for God. Like Jacob DeShazer, we face our enemies every day. And one of the greatest enemies every Christian must face is the enemy called fear.

Our fears erode our confidence and keep us from stepping out boldly for the Lord. Fear comes into our souls as a raging storm, a storm that assaults our faith, leaving us cowering and paralyzed. But Jesus is with us amid the storm. He speaks peace to our hearts. He calms our fears. He restores our souls.

Jesus Rebukes the Storm

This passage, Mark 4:35–5:20, presents us with two incidents: the stilling of the storm on the Sea of Galilee and, immediately following that, the healing of a demonized man. Both incidents deal with the problem of fear and how to respond to it. The Scriptures often deal with the subject of fear because fear is the common experience of all humanity. Mark begins his discussion of fear by providing us with this background regarding the incident of the storm on the Sea of Galilee.

> *That day when evening came, he said to his disciples,*
> *"Let us go over to the other side." Leaving the crowd behind,*
> *they took him along, just as he was, in the boat. There were*
> *also other boats with him.* (MARK 4:35–36)

This incident begins when our Lord is at the point of utter physical exhaustion. We are still in that section of Mark in which he emphasizes several incidents that underscore Jesus' growing popularity. Jesus is beset by crowds everywhere He turns, work that leaves Him physically exhausted and emotionally spent. We find Him at the end of a heavy day of teaching, ministering, and healing. Soul-weary, He steps into the boat and tells the disciples, "Let's get away. Let's move to the other side of the lake." The eastern shore of the lake is about five miles away. Mark makes clear that this was unpremeditated on Jesus' part: "They took him along, just as he was, in the boat." Jesus had made no preparation for this journey.

Mark also indicates that witnesses were present to testify to the strange thing that happened next: "There were also other boats with him." Mark adds this statement to attest that what happened during the journey was not a hallucination. A liberal Bible commentator once suggested that there was no literal calming of the storm. Instead, he claimed, our Lord merely settled the disciples' fear. It was not the wind and waves but merely their hearts that Jesus stilled. According to this theory, the disciples only thought they witnessed a miracle. But this explanation ignores the fact that other people in nearby boats also witnessed and testified to this miracle. Here is how Mark describes the incident:

> *A furious squall came up, and the waves broke over the boat, so that it was nearly swamped. Jesus was in the stern, sleeping on a cushion. The disciples woke him and said to him, "Teacher, don't you care if we drown?"*
>
> *He got up, rebuked the wind and said to the waves, "Quiet! Be still!" Then the wind died down and it was completely calm.* (MARK 4:37–39)

As Mark relates the drama, a raging storm comes suddenly on the sea. Such weather conditions still occur in the rugged country around the northeast portion of the Sea of Galilee, an area known today as the Golan Heights. In that terrain, the winds often gather and break suddenly on the sea, causing a violent storm to arise in a matter of minutes.

That is the kind of storm the disciples encounter soon after they set out toward the eastern shore. Within moments the sea is lashed by winds, so that great waves mount up. The boat fills with water as waves crash over the bow. Although they are experienced sailors, the disciples panic. This storm exceeds all their experience, and they believe they are going to die. So they go to the back of the boat and wake Jesus, asking, "Teacher, don't you care if we drown?" Matthew's account adds this bit of dialogue: "Lord, save us! We're going to drown!" (Matthew 8:25).

In the midst of this growing peril, Jesus has gone to sleep. The disciples awaken Jesus not only because they are afraid of the storm but also because they are upset over the Lord's seeming indifference to their need. Maybe you can identify with the disciples. You may be caught in a stormy experience. You face extreme danger. You call out to the Lord, and He seems unaware, unconcerned, perhaps even asleep. Your situation frightens you, but God's seeming indifference angers you. You cry out, and there is no answer. So you begin to panic. That is the situation here.

After they had awakened Him, our Lord arose, and at first He said nothing to the disciples. Instead, He rebuked the wind. The sense of the Greek is that He muzzled the sea.

It's interesting to wonder what the disciples had expected Jesus to do when they said, "Lord, save us!" and "Don't you care if we drown?" They didn't expect Him to do what He did. When He commanded the wind and waves, and the storm obeyed Him, they were shocked. But prior to that moment, they were filled with fear. It is this attitude of fear, which is just another word for faithlessness, that Jesus rebukes.

Let's take a closer look at the miracle that Jesus performed. The miracle does not lie in the calming of the storm, for nature would have done so eventually. The miracle had to do with the suddenness with which it happened. With one command from Jesus, the wind that had lashed their boat and roared in their ears fell to less than a whisper. The waves that had swamped their boat settled to a glassy calm. In that moment, the disciples knew they were in the presence of an authority beyond their imagining.

When the account says that the Lord rebuked the wind and spoke to the sea, we need to understand that He was not really speaking to the elements. What good does it do to talk to the air as it flows by or to the water as it rages?

I am reminded of the story of the Danish king, Canute, who reigned nearly a thousand years ago. The noblemen who served

King Canute were overly fond of flattering him with extravagant praise for his power and majesty. So, to shut them up, he ordered that his throne be taken down to the seashore. There, he sat on his throne and commanded the tide not to come in. Again and again, he commanded the sea, yet the waves kept crashing closer and closer to the throne. Eventually they washed over throne and king. The noblemen rushed into the waves and pulled their king to safety. After that incident, King Canute refused to wear his crown. Instead, he placed it on a statue of the crucified Christ.

The wind and the sea have no mind, no will to either obey or disobey. So I don't believe our Lord was really speaking to the elements of air and sea. We must remember that Jesus knew well what is invisible: the forces of the demonic realm. I believe that storm was stirred up by demonic forces, and it was those evil spirits that Jesus commanded to be still.

We must never forget that we live in a fallen world. Scriptures tell us that our planet is in the grip of the devil and his agents. The disasters we read of or experience are frequently the result of Satan's attack on humanity: earthquakes, famines, floods, droughts, cyclones, tornadoes, and hurricanes. Jesus understood this, and he rebuked not the wind but the evil one, who had awakened the wind. Jesus lived in the constant realization that, as the apostle Paul has written, "our struggle is not against flesh and blood, but against the rulers, against the authorities, against the powers of this dark world and against the spiritual forces of evil in the heavenly realms" (Ephesians 6:12).

This view was suggested to me when I noticed that the words Jesus used to rebuke the storm are the same words He used to rebuke the demon that interrupted His discourse in the synagogue at Capernaum (see Mark 1:23–28). So it seems clear that when Jesus speaks peace to the storm, He is truly addressing the unseen, invisible world.

Jesus Rebukes His Disciples

After Jesus rebukes the wind and the sea, He turns and gives another stinging rebuke, this time to His disciples: "Why are you so afraid? Do you still have no faith?" (Mark 4:40).

Notice that first question: "Why are you so afraid?" Isn't that a strange question to ask men who were, moments before, in the middle of a raging storm? The wind was shrieking. The sea was filling their boat. They had no visible hope of rescue. Why shouldn't they be afraid? If you and I had been in their place, would we have reacted any differently?

But then notice His second question: "Do you still have no faith?" For that was the real issue, wasn't it? The reason these disciples were filled with fear is the same reason all people, you and I included, become afraid· we lose faith. Faith is the answer to fear. Where there is faith, there is no fear. When fear reigns, faith has fled. These disciples were full of fear because they had no faith. They had forgotten what Jesus had told them in the Sermon on the Mount: "If that is how God clothes the grass of the field, which is here today and tomorrow is thrown into the fire, will he not much more clothe you, O you of little faith?" (Matthew 6:30). They had forgotten what He had taught about God's love and provision.

How would the disciples have acted if they had demonstrated faith? For one thing, they would not have awakened Jesus; they would have let Him rest. He was weary and tired and needed the rest. They would have done so because their faith would have reminded them of two great facts. The boat will not sink; it cannot sink when the Master of ocean, earth, and sky is aboard. And the storm will not last forever.

The Storm Will Not Last Forever

A good friend of mine, a young evangelist from another country, once unburdened himself to me about some trials he and his wife were experiencing. She was struggling with severe physical problems involving asthma and bronchitis. They had gone through years of struggle with this condition, and it hindered not only her health but also his effectiveness in ministry. As they were planning to return to their country, she became acutely sick again. He had come to me for counsel, encouragement, and prayer.

As we talked, I took my Bible and turned to this incident in Mark. "I would encourage you to keep two truths in mind throughout this time of trial," I said. "First, the boat will not sink. Second, the storm will not last forever. That's what it means to have faith through a crisis."

He thanked me, we prayed together, and he left. A couple of months later, we got together once more. "How are things going?" I asked. "How is your wife?"

"Oh, not much better," he replied. "She's still having terrible struggles. She can't breathe, and she can't take care of the children or the house. We're going through a very difficult time, but I always remember two things: the boat will not sink, and the storm will not last forever!" So I prayed with him again.

More months passed, and I received a note from him. A doctor had discovered a minor deficiency in the wife's diet. Once that deficiency was remedied, the asthma and bronchitis disappeared. After that, she was in glorious, radiant health, and they were rejoicing together. At the bottom of that note, he closed with these words: "The boat will not sink, and the storm will not last forever."

Faith is the answer to fear—faith in the goodness and care of God for our lives. That is one lesson we can take away from this story, but still another lesson is embedded here. It is the lesson that the failure of faith can often open a doorway to greater vision. Read on as Mark continues:

> *They were terrified and asked each other, "Who is this?*
> *Even the wind and the waves obey him!"* (MARK 4:41)

The disciples were terrified. They were filled with fear, but it is a different kind of fear than their earlier fear. Before, they felt a cowardly fear. Now they are filled with a terror that is akin to awe and worship. Out of the failure of their faith came a deeper insight, a glimpse into the mystery of Jesus' personhood and godhood. They had seen Him heal the sick and cast out demons. They had known He was someone special, but they hadn't begun to plumb the depths of who Jesus was: the great I AM. Now, as He demonstrates authority over the wind and sea, they find themselves in the presence of a deep mystery, and they are filled with a terrified awe, as well they should be!

And so they ask each other, "Who is this? Even the wind and the waves obey him!" The wonderful thing about this incident is that even though the disciples flunked their examination of faith, the groundwork was laid for a new and deeper understanding of faith. Their failure opened the possibility for a new expression of faith to come.

This is the way God works in our lives. He tests our faith in order that we might grow. As our faith grows, we see that He is able to handle each problem in our lives. Even if our faith is weak, He still will not let us collapse. He will hold us up and see us through, and in the process He will lay the foundation for a new glimpse of His might and power.

The Man Among the Tombs

The calming of the storm at the end of Mark 4 was the first incident in which Jesus deals with our fears. Now, as we move into Mark 5, we are introduced to the second incident relating to our fears and our faith. Mark writes:

> They went across the lake to the region of the Gerasenes. When Jesus got out of the boat, a man with an evil [or, more literally, unclean] spirit came from the tombs to meet him. This man lived in the tombs, and no one could bind him any more, not even with a chain. For he had often been chained hand and foot, but he tore the chains apart and broke the irons on his feet. No one was strong enough to subdue him. Night and day among the tombs and in the hills he would cry out and cut himself with stones.
>
> When he saw Jesus from a distance, he ran and fell on his knees in front of him. He shouted at the top of his voice, "What do you want with me, Jesus, Son of the Most High God? Swear to God that you won't torture me!" For Jesus had said to him, "Come out of this man, you evil spirit!"
>
> Then Jesus asked him, "What is your name?"
>
> "My name is Legion," he replied, "for we are many." And he begged Jesus again and again not to send them out of the area.
>
> A large herd of pigs was feeding on the nearby hillside. The demons begged Jesus, "Send us among the pigs; allow us to go into them." He gave them permission, and the evil spirits came out and went into the pigs. The herd, about two thousand in number, rushed down the steep bank into the lake and were drowned. (MARK 5:1–13)

This incident opens again the whole realm of the occult, the demonic, and the oppression of humankind by unclean spirits. This account presents us with a remarkable listing of the signs of a person who is demonized or, in popular terminology, demon-possessed. It is evident that there are various stages and degrees to which evil spirits can affect and even control human beings. In this incident we have an extreme case, and Mark lists seven signs that indicate when demonic spirits are at work in the life of an individual.

The first sign is the word "unclean." There is always an element of the unclean present in demonic activity. Demonic uncleanness may involve moral pollution, or it may even involve physical filth. In this case, the man lived among the tombs, that is, among the dead bodies in the limestone caves in the cliffs along the Sea of Galilee. It is no accident that the rise of satanism and occultism in our culture is accompanied by the spread of pornography, obscenity, and an obsession with death, horror, and torture in our entertainment media.

The second sign is that the man lived in isolation. He had a home, and he had friends, because Jesus sent him back to both at the end of the story. But he chose to live by himself in utter loneliness. Demonic influence is characterized by this attitude of withdrawal, a willingness to be physically and emotionally separate from other people.

The third sign was the man's supernatural strength. This is often the case among demonized people. There are many instances of people possessed or controlled by demons exercising unusual strength. This man had been bound with chains and fetters, but he had snapped the chains and torn off the fetters, and no one had the strength to subdue him. This is a clear and remarkable demonstration of demonic power.

The fourth sign was the sense of torment. At first, demonic influence can seem alluring, seductive, and pleasurable. But that is designed to lead one deeper and deeper into realm of the demonic until the torment sets in. This man's torment was demonstrated by his deep sense of restlessness, in which he wandered up and down the mountains, crying out in pain, bruising and cutting himself with stones, in a useless attempt to drive out his inner torment. This is characteristic of demonic influence.

The fifth sign was the immediate recognition of the authority of Jesus. This man immediately knew who Jesus was. He ran to Him and called Him by name, using the phrase the demons always employ: "Son of the Most High God." This is revealing, because it is the highest name a nonbeliever can use in reference to God. All through the Old Testament, members of the Gentile nations use this name when they speak of God. Israel knew Him as Jehovah, or "Lord." But the rest of the world knew Him as El Elyon, "God Most High." This is how the demons refer to Him.

The sixth sign is the duality or multiplicity of personalities seen in this man. When Jesus asked him, "What is your name?" the demonized man replies, "My name is Legion, for we are many."

The seventh and final sign is a tendency to self-destruction. I want to make it absolutely clear that not all suicidal people are demonized. Many people suffer from suicidal depression due to natural causes, including treatable medical conditions. Suicidal tendencies should never be taken in isolation as an indication that a person is demonized. But it is important to note that demonized people are often self-destructive.

In this incident, Jesus cast the demons out of the man. And what did the demons do? All two thousand of them rushed down the mountainside and drowned themselves in the sea. Thus the demons, who had asked to enter the pigs in order not to go into the abyss, defeated their purpose. When the pigs were drowned, the demons descended into the abyss anyway, and that is why Jesus gave them permission to enter into the pigs. The death of the pigs was a powerful testimony to this man that he was free from the demons that had inhabited him. But it was also the means by which these demons were sent into the abyss, where they belonged.

The Sequel to the Story

Mark next records a strange reaction on the part of the people in that region. Their reaction forms the sequel to the story.

> *Those tending the pigs ran off and reported this in the town and countryside, and the people went out to see what had happened. When they came to Jesus, they saw the man who had been possessed by the legion of demons, sitting there, dressed and in his right mind; and they were afraid. Those who had seen it told the people what had happened to the demon-possessed man—and told about the pigs as well. Then the people began to plead with Jesus to leave their region.* (MARK 5:14–17)

The herdsmen had just seen an incredible thing. Their entire herd of pigs had drowned themselves. So they went to the town and around the countryside and told the people of the region what had happened. The people rushed out and found the formerly demonized man sitting clothed and in his right mind. He was sitting at the feet of Jesus, listening attentively. They saw that this man had been delivered and set free. And were their hearts gladdened by what they saw?

No. In fact, they begged Jesus to leave. They would rather have a crazed man inhabited by demons in their midst than Jesus Himself. Why?

Jesus had just hit these people in the tenderest part of their anatomy: their pocketbook. Pigs, remember, were a ceremonially unclean animal to the Jews; the law of Moses forbade the eating of pork. Yet pigs were important to the economy of the region. Perhaps pigs were raised to be sold to the Romans who occupied the land. In any case, a huge profit drowned in the sea when Jesus sent the demons into that herd of pigs. That is why, instead of rejoicing that a man was healed and restored to his right mind, these people pleaded with Jesus to go away.

Jesus, who is above all a gentleman, does not stay where He is not welcome. He was asked to leave, so He left. Mark's account continues:

> As Jesus was getting into the boat, the man who had been demon-possessed begged to go with him. Jesus did not let him, but said, "Go home to your family and tell them how much the Lord has done for you, and how he has had mercy on you." So the man went away and began to tell in the Decapolis how much Jesus had done for him. And all the people were amazed. (MARK 5:18–20)

The Decapolis was a cluster of ten Greek cities on the eastern side of the Sea of Galilee. One of these cities was Damascus, the capital of modern-day Syria. Jesus commanded the delivered man to go to that Gentile community and bear witness of the transformation in his life. Jesus did not tell the man to go door to door but to tell his friends what happened to him. That is what witnesses do. They tell what they have seen or experienced. Here we see a distinction between witnessing and evangelism. A witness says, "Here is how God changed my life," whereas an evangelist preaches the good news and says, "Here is how God can change your life."

This man was sent to be a witness, to tell people what had happened to him. And what a story he had to tell! He had lived in anguish and torment, alone and isolated, a menace to himself and to people around him. Then Jesus came and delivered him. Because of Jesus, the man was free, full of joy, and in his right mind. No wonder everyone who heard him marveled at his story.

What is the significance for our lives of these two incidents from the life of Jesus? Mark has put them together to help us see that Jesus is Lord of all our circumstances. No matter what circumstances arise to frighten us, subvert us, or sabotage us— whether an external enemy, or an internal force such as a sinful habit or unhealthy attitude, or even a demonic influence that seeks to destroy us—Jesus is the Lord. When we have faith in Him, there is no room for fear. Faith and fear cannot coexist within us. One or the other will reign in us.

So the question Jesus asks us is the same question He put to His disciples in the calm after the storm: "Why are you so afraid? Do you still have no faith?"

ten

The Weakness of the World

> **Mark 5:21–6:6**

Years ago, when our daughter Susan was little, our family was driving through a sparsely populated area in Oregon. During our motel stay the previous night, Susan had developed a fever, but it didn't seem serious. As we drove along this remote stretch of highway, Susan suddenly went into convulsions in her mother's arms. Her eyes turned up, and her body began to spasm. It was a frightening thing to watch, and our child was in great danger.

My heart pounded with fear as I pulled the car over, took Susan from her mother's arms, and rushed across the road to a farmhouse. It was early, about six in the morning, but it was no time to be considerate of anyone's sleep. My fist thundered on the door. A woman answered, and I said, "My daughter is very sick. She's in convulsions! Do you have a bathtub where we can put her in warm water?"

The woman was so taken aback she hardly knew what to say. She motioned down the hall, and I rushed past her, found the bathroom, and started running water in the tub. We found out later that this family had the only bathtub and the only phone for miles around. I felt that God had led me to that farmhouse. We called a doctor and arranged to take the baby to him.

In the end, Susan came through all right, and so did my wife and I. But I have never forgotten that terrible moment when I thought my daughter might die in my arms. I have never felt so weak, so powerless, so helpless.

I believe that incident gave me a sense of what was going through the minds of the people we are about to meet in the latter half of Mark 5 and the first few verses of Mark 6. We will look at three incidents in the life of Jesus, the Servant of God. In the process, we will see one theme that threads its way throughout the story of the raising of the daughter of Jairus, the healing of the woman with an ongoing flow of blood, and the second visit of Jesus to His hometown, Nazareth. The theme we will examine is that of the weakness of the world. Put another way, this section deals with the impotence of nature, the inability of natural life to meet the needs of suffering hearts.

A Father's Agonized Plea

The incidents in this section bring to a close the third major division of the gospel of Mark. The first division, Mark 1:1–39, portrays the theme of the authority of the Servant. The second division, Mark 1:40–3:6, show us His penetrating, insightful knowledge of our humanity. The third division, Mark 3:7–6:6, which this study brings to a close, portrays for us the immense popularity of our Lord and His ministry and the problems and hindrances caused by His popularity.

We are witnessing the season of our Lord's greatest popularity, when people came to Him from all over the land—north, east, south, and west—from within the borders of Israel and even beyond those borders. People thronged to Him and pressed on Him and pursued Him everywhere He went. His popularity awakened human opposition, demonic opposition, unreasonable expectations, misunderstanding about His purpose in the world, simple human exhaustion, and more.

With this as our background, we come to the intertwined stories of two sufferers: Jairus, the ruler of the synagogue, whose problem was fear and sorrow at the death of his daughter; and the woman who had spent twelve years enduring the pain and distress of a continuous flow of blood. We look first at the approach of Jairus.

> *When Jesus had again crossed over by boat to the other side of the lake, a large crowd gathered around him while he was by the lake. Then one of the synagogue rulers, named Jairus, came there. Seeing Jesus, he fell at his feet and pleaded earnestly with him, "My little daughter is dying. Please come and put your hands on her so that she will be healed and live." So Jesus went with him.*
>
> *A large crowd followed and pressed around him.*
>
> (MARK 5:21–24)

It must have been difficult for Jairus to come to Jesus. He was one of the rulers of the synagogue, and his religious colleagues undoubtedly disapproved of his having any contact with Jesus of Nazareth. At this time, the synagogues were practically closed to the ministry of Jesus. He had healed so many people on the Sabbath day and had offended the Pharisees so greatly that they had cut Him off from ministry within the synagogue.

So Jesus was preaching in the open countryside, and He was approached by the ruler of the most prominent synagogue in Capernaum. "My little daughter is dying," said the man. What did this man have to overcome in order to say those words to Jesus? Pride? Prejudice? Embarrassment? Fear of what others might say or do to him? Yet, as I can testify, when your daughter's life is on the line, you can think of nothing but getting the help she needs. So Jairus went to this itinerant teacher who was so hated by the leading scholars of the time, and he fell at Jesus' feet and begged Him for mercy.

Fear drove Jairus to Jesus. The man's daughter had filled his home with sunshine for twelve years, and now she was about to be taken from him. But is parental fear all that motivated Jairus? No. Mark is careful to show us that this man was also motivated by faith. "Please come," Jairus pleaded, "and put your hands on her so that she will be healed and live." Although he was of the group of religious leaders who had opposed Jesus, Jairus was not like them. He believed that there was power in Jesus, and faith drove him to the feet of Jesus. His pride and prejudice forgotten, Jairus went to the Lord and pleaded for help.

One Story Interrupts Another

Our Lord responded instantly to this father's anguish and went with him. But at this point, Mark turns to an interruption that arose as Jesus and Jairus were on their way to the house. They had not gotten far before they were stopped by a woman, and it is interesting to notice a common denominator between these two intertwined stories. That common denominator is the number twelve. The woman whom Jesus met had suffered from a flow of blood for twelve years; the daughter of Jairus was twelve years old, a fact that is revealed later (Mark 5:42). What is the significance of the number twelve?

In the Bible, the number twelve and major multiples of twelve, such as 144 or 12,000 or 144,000, are usually symbolic of God's people, Israel, and of the true church of Jesus Christ. In the Old Testament, we see that Jacob had twelve sons, and their descendents became the twelve tribes of Israel. In the New Testament, Jesus chose twelve apostles. At the feeding of the five thousand (Mark 6), twelve baskets of leftover food were collected. In Revelation 21, we are shown the holy city, the new Jerusalem, coming down from heaven, with twelve gates inscribed with the names of the twelve tribes of Israel, and twelve foundations with the names of the twelve apostles inscribed thereon. The holy city measures 12,000 stadia cubed, and its walls are 144 cubits thick. The symbol of an even dozen is significant to God, for it stands for God's people—His chosen people in the Old Testament and His elect in the New Testament.

It may be that the number twelve, associated with a sick Jewish woman and a dying Jewish girl, suggests the suffering and death that God's people are subject to until, by faith, they receive the healing, life-giving touch of Jesus. Let us read Mark's account of the meeting between Jesus and the suffering woman.

A woman was there who had been subject to bleeding for twelve years. She had suffered a great deal under the care of many doctors and had spent all she had, yet instead of getting better she grew worse. (MARK 5:25–26)

Mark tells us three things about this woman: her condition, her cure, and her confession before Jesus. First, let's look at her condition. She was suffering from what doctors would call a vaginal hemorrhage, a continual flow of blood that not only gave her great distress and pain but also rendered her ceremonially unclean. Because of this, she was ostracized from Jewish society. She had to keep her distance from everyone, almost as if she were a leper. People were forbidden to touch her while she was in this condition, and she could not attend services in the temple or synagogue. For twelve years she had been denied all the comfort and solace of her community and her faith. She was alone and anguished because of a continual flow of blood.

To make matters worse, she had spent all her money on doctors, and they had not only failed to cure her, but she had become even more ill. Mark seems to imply that none of those doctors had the grace to tell her they couldn't help her. They just kept taking her money. But when she came to Jesus, something wonderful happened.

> When she heard about Jesus, she came up behind him in the crowd and touched his cloak, because she thought, "If I just touch his clothes, I will be healed." Immediately her bleeding stopped and she felt in her body that she was freed from her suffering. (MARK 5:27–29)

Word had reached this suffering woman that a man had come who had the power to heal. When her hopes were awakened, her faith was stirred, and she became convinced that Jesus could help her. But this woman had a problem. She was ceremonially unclean; it was a violation of the law of Moses for her to get close to anyone or talk to anyone. So she had to come to Jesus by an unusual route. She thought, *It would be wrong for Him to touch me, but if I could just touch Him, I would be made well!* So, as the crowd pressed in around Him, she pushed her way close to Him until she could touch Him. But no, she dared not touch Jesus—only the hem of His cloak. Just one touch of His clothes, she believed, would be enough.

She reached out. Her fingers brushed the hem, the very edge, of the robe Jesus wore. Instantly she felt the healing power of Jesus invade her body. The flow of blood stopped at that moment. The woman knew she was healed. Mark describes that scene.

> At once Jesus realized that power had gone out from
> him. He turned around in the crowd and asked, "Who
> touched my clothes?"
>   "You see the people crowding against you," his disciples
> answered, "and yet you can ask, 'Who touched me?'"
>   But Jesus kept looking around to see who had done it.
> Then the woman, knowing what had happened to her, came
> and fell at his feet and, trembling with fear, told him the
> whole truth. He said to her, "Daughter, your faith has healed
> you. Go in peace and be freed from your suffering."
>   (MARK 5:30–34)

That is a wonderful picture of faith. Scores of people undoubtedly touched Jesus as He walked along toward the house of Jairus. As the disciples pointed out to Him, the people pressed Him and jostled Him from every side. But only one woman reached out in genuine faith and touched Him. The others may have bumped Him, tapped Him on the shoulder, or even grabbed His arm, but they received nothing from Him. Only this one woman received healing power.

This story indicates something of what the healing ministry of Jesus cost Him. At the woman's touch, He felt power go forth from Him. He felt weaker. Jesus paid a personal price whenever He reached out to heal someone. No wonder He was physically exhausted at the end of the day. Power was going out from Him every day. It was a demanding ministry.

This incident also shows that the healing work was performed by God the Father, not by Jesus. Even though our Lord felt the healing power flow out of Him, He did not will the healing to take place, for He didn't know who had touched Him. Without His choosing or awareness, the touch of faith drew from

Him the power to heal—the power of God the Father. This is confirmation of what Jesus tells us: "The words I say to you are not just my own. Rather, it is the Father, living in me, who is doing his work" (John 14:10). An all-seeing God watched this woman push her way through the crowd, saw the faith in her heart, and responded by sending His power to her via the life of Jesus.

Having said that, however, we must acknowledge that Jesus had some part in this healing, because when the woman fell down before Him and told the whole truth, He said to her, "Daughter, your faith has healed you. Go in peace and be freed from your suffering." When He says, "Your faith has healed you," the verb tense in the Greek means "be continually healed." In other words, Jesus graciously granted her a continuance in good health.

This is the only time recorded in the Scriptures that Jesus ever used the term "daughter." Jesus dealt tenderly with this woman because, despite her shame and embarrassment, she blurted out the truth in front of the crowd. I think that is the ground on which Jesus granted her continual healing: she told Him the truth. When He asked who had touched Him, she fell down before Him, told Him all about her problem, and put the problem in His hands. What if she had not responded so honestly? What if she had tried instead to lose herself in the crowd and seek anonymity? It may be that she would have had her disease back in hours. And that may help explain why some purported healings in our day fail.

Back to the Story of Jairus . . .

At this point, Mark returns us to the story of Jairus and his sick twelve-year-old daughter. Mark writes:

While Jesus was still speaking, some men came from the house of Jairus, the synagogue ruler. "Your daughter is dead," they said. "Why bother the teacher any more?"

Ignoring what they said, Jesus told the synagogue ruler, "Don't be afraid; just believe."

He did not let anyone follow him except Peter, James and John the brother of James. When they came to the home of the synagogue ruler, Jesus saw a commotion, with people crying and wailing loudly. He went in and said to them, "Why all this commotion and wailing? The child is not dead but asleep." But they laughed at him . . . (MARK 5:35–40)

This account serves to underscore the finality and awfulness of death. Here we see the point where human efforts end and death takes over. Perhaps you have been present when doctors have made an emergency effort to revive a patient. The moment the vital signs have ceased, the emergency personnel become intensely, frantically focused on efforts to revive the patient. When they are successful, there is great relief all around. But in those cases where the patient does not respond, a moment eventually comes when the doctors say, "He's gone," and all work stops. The emergency equipment is packed up. The body is covered and taken away. There is finality in that moment; death has set in.

You sense that same feeling of finality at a funeral, when the loved ones walk away from the graveside of a loved one. The body is consigned to the earth, and the survivors must learn to live with their loss. That is the sense of finality we find in this story. Imagine how Jairus must feel as Jesus deals with the woman who had touched Him. Jairus didn't want to interrupt the Lord, yet his daughter was dying.

But even as Jesus is speaking, messengers arrive from the house of Jairus. "Your daughter is dead," they tell him, and his heart is shattered. Still, Jesus tells Jairus, "Don't be afraid; just believe." Again we see that fear is to be met by faith. "Trust in God" is the only answer to fear.

It is interesting to notice those whom Jesus takes with Him. He wants them to witness something they will never forget. From this moment on in Mark's account, we will see Peter's first-person testimony of these events woven throughout Mark's gospel.

As Jesus and Jairus approach the house, they hear that the mourners have already begun their wailing cry. It was customary in those days (and this custom still exists in parts of the Middle East) to hire mourners to bemoan the death of an individual. The mourners would rip their garments, tear out their hair, and cry out with shrieks and howls. Although there is a seeming insincerity about the practice, these professional mourners did authentically portray the terrible sense of despair that people felt and still feel in the face of death.

Encountering the noisy weeping of the mourners, Jesus says, "Why all this commotion and wailing? The child is not dead but asleep." For a moment, the mourners seem to forget how they are to behave when someone has died. They pause from their weeping and wailing long enough to laugh scornfully at Jesus. We can understand their laughter, because it is absurd to suppose that a dead person is merely sleeping.

And yet, who has the truer view of death, Jesus or mere human beings like ourselves? You may recall that Jesus says much the same thing when He is told that Lazarus has died. "Our friend Lazarus has fallen asleep," the Lord replied, "but I am going there to wake him up" (John 11:11). Again and again, Jesus refers to death as a sleep when it involves a believer.

A New View of Sickness and Death

As Mark continues the account, we are about to gain a new and clearer view of the weakness of this world in which we daily wage a losing battle against sickness and death.

> *After he put them all out, he took the child's father and mother and the disciples who were with him, and went in where the child was. He took her by the hand and said to her, "Talitha koum!" (which means, "Little girl, I say to you, get up!"). Immediately the girl stood up and walked around (she was twelve years old). At this they were completely astonished.* (MARK 5:40–42)

Notice that Jesus first puts all the people out of the house except the father and mother, and Peter and James and John. Then they go into the place where the child's body lies. The parents are brokenhearted, but Jesus walks to the side of the little girl and, taking her by the hand, says in Aramaic, "Talitha koum," or, literally, "Little girl, little lamb, arise." Peter was present to hear those words, and he never forgot them. Mark preserves these words of Jesus in Aramaic, just as He had spoken them and just as Peter recalled them.

Wherever that child's spirit had gone, she heard the words of Jesus and she obeyed, reuniting with her body. Instantly health and strength came back into her, and she arose and walked around the room, to the amazement of all who were there.

Mark next records a touching detail. Jesus said, "Give her something to eat." Peter was amazed that the Lord Jesus would think so tenderly of her as to remember her need for food after such an ordeal.

Why did Jesus raise this child? He didn't do it for the little girl's sake. Remember, He called her back to a life of pain, struggle, worry, and heartache. Someday she would have to face death again. By bringing this girl back to life and calling her away from a pleasant sleep in the arms of God, Jesus did her no favors. He didn't raise the child for her sake but for the sake of Jairus and his wife, to assuage the agony of their loss.

You may say, "Well, that's a nice story, but Jesus has never done that for me. I am sick, and He hasn't healed me. I have lost a loved one, and He has not taken away my grief. I am facing death, and I don't expect Him to walk into my house and raise me out of my deathbed." And all of that may well be true. Why, then, doesn't Jesus respond to our hurt and death and loss as He responded so long ago?

I believe that Jesus did not want us to expect to be healed and restored as the woman and the child were. He specifically wants to discourage any such expectations. We know this because He told people not to tell anyone about these events.

> *He gave strict orders not to let anyone know about this,*
> *and told them to give her something to eat.* (MARK 5:43)

Jesus did not want this news broadcast, because He didn't want to be invited to every funeral in Palestine. The lesson we are to learn from the healing of the woman and the raising of Jairus's daughter is not, "You can be restored in the same way," but rather, "Here is how you should view sickness and death." It is a message to us about the weakness of this world and the weakness of our humanity.

Our bodies are temporary, fragile, and subject to death and corruption. From the moment we are born, we begin to die. Doctors and medicines, exercise and good nutrition may stave off the inevitable for a few weeks, months, or even years. But we cannot place our trust in this world, which is too weak and corrupt to save us. We must place our trust in God, not in the weak things of this world.

Limited Views Produce Limited Lives

Dr. G. Campbell Morgan, the great English expositor of Scripture and a man who has taught me much about the Christian faith through his writings, once compared the raising of Jairus's daughter with the loss of his firstborn daughter. He wrote:

> I can hardly speak of this matter without becoming personal and reminiscent, remembering a time forty years ago when my own first lassie lay at the point of death, dying. I called for Him then, and He came, and surely said to our troubled hearts, "Fear not, believe only." He did not say, "She shall be made whole." She was not made whole, on the earthly plane; she passed away into the life beyond. But He did say to her, "Talitha cumi," i.e., "Little lamb, arise." But in her case that did not mean, "Stay on the earth level"; it meant that He needed her, and He took her to be with Himself. She has been with Him for all these years, as we measure time here, and I have missed her every day. But His word, "Believe only," has been the strength of all the passing years.

This is the perspective Jesus intends for us to learn from the story of Jairus's daughter. He wants us to know that He is able to bring wholeness to our suffering hearts, even though the world's resources have been exhausted. This truth is highlighted for us in the brief account we have next, in the opening words of Mark 6:

Jesus left there and went to his hometown, accompanied by his disciples. When the Sabbath came, he began to teach in the synagogue, and many who heard him were amazed.

"Where did this man get these things?" they asked. "What's this wisdom that has been given him, that he even does miracles! Isn't this the carpenter? Isn't this Mary's son and the brother of James, Joseph, Judas and Simon? Aren't his sisters here with us?" And they took offense at him.

Jesus said to them, "Only in his hometown, among his relatives and in his own house is a prophet without honor." He could not do any miracles there, except lay his hands on a few sick people and heal them. And he was amazed at their lack of faith.

Then Jesus went around teaching from village to village. (MARK 6:1–6)

We can gather up the meaning of this account in a few words: limited views produce limited lives. If your view of life is narrow and confined only to what you can detect with your five senses, then your life is going to be limited and spiritually impoverished.

This is how it was in Nazareth. Jesus had been reared in Nazareth, and He was well known there. Now He comes back and teaches in the synagogue, and people are astonished. They ask the right questions: "Where did this man get these things? What's this wisdom that has been given him, that he even does miracles!"

But the answers to their questions are limited. "Isn't this the carpenter? Isn't this Mary's son and the brother of James, Joseph, Judas and Simon? Aren't his sisters here with us?" Some of these people eat off of tables or sit in chairs Jesus built for them. They know His brothers and sisters. They know the whole family. They watched Him grow up. How can this be the miracle worker, the great teacher they have heard about?

In the end, they took refuge in that final resort of all small minds. They ridiculed Him. They discounted all He had done, and they said, "He can't be anything, because we know Him. We know His beginnings, His family, where He came from."

So Jesus pointed out to them that this is characteristic of fallen human nature. There is no recognition of His worth in His hometown. And for the town of Nazareth, there is a price to pay for unbelief. No mighty work is done there. And although Nazareth has never been forgotten as the town in which Jesus grew up, to this day it is regarded in Palestine with some sense of embarrassment. Nothing honorable has ever been associated with Nazareth, other than the fact that Jesus grew up there. The town had missed its one great opportunity.

The message of this account is clear. Do not restrict your vision. Instead, lift up your eyes and look beyond the visible to all the unimaginable realities of God. Live life to its fullest dimensions, as God intended it to be lived. Life can never be explained merely in terms of the natural. The resources of the natural world are weak and finite; they come to an end. But God is rich in grace and rich in power. His resources are immense and infinite. His word to us is, "Don't be afraid; just believe."

eleven

"Who Is This?"

➤ **Mark 6:7–52**

As a young man, Kaezad Dadachanjee used to meditate for several hours a day in a temple dedicated to the fire god, Ahura Mazda. He lived in a south Asian country and was a member of the Parsi sect, which claims a direct lineage from the ancient Persians and the Zoroastrian religion. But young Kaezad was deeply troubled and had many questions about his religion that the Parsi scholars could not answer. One question that troubled him was the object of Parsi worship. *Why do we worship fire?* he thought. *Wouldn't it make more sense to worship a creator than to worship a created thing?*

As he meditated at the temple of fire, Kaezad found he could no longer pray to Ahura Mazda. While the others of his sect knelt toward the sacred fire, he chose to face a different direction. He addressed his prayers to a different God and an unknown Creator, and he asked this unknown God to reveal Himself. Eventually, in search of a better life, Kaezad left his country and moved to the United States. He studied science, mathematics, and computers at an American university, and he visited various Christian churches in his search for the unknown Creator.

Kaezad was living in Arlington, Texas, when his neighbors struck up a conversation with him as he sat outside, reading the Parsi holy writings. This Christian couple invited Kaezad to their home for dinner and gave him a Bible to keep. Not long afterward, they invited him to church, where he heard the message of salvation by grace through faith in Jesus Christ. "I found answers," he recalls, "when I found Jesus."

After his encounter with Christ, Kaezad felt an overwhelming burden to evangelize the two million people in the worldwide Parsi community. His burden was so heavy that he often wept as he prayed for his people. He knew they were lost without Christ, and no one was taking the gospel to them. Soon Kaezad sensed that God was calling him to become a missionary to the Parsi people. In response to that call, he founded the Love Parsi ministry and helped produce a Parsi translation of the Bible.

During one of Kaezad's ministry trips to his homeland, he was walking in a rural area when he saw a man running toward him. The man wore religious garb and held an object used for casting magical spells. "Immediately anger rose up within me," Kaezad recalls, "not toward the man, because he needed salvation, but anger toward the devil." The man was trying to launch a spiritual attack against Kaezad, employing the devil's sorcerous arts against him. But Kaezad responded by saying to the man, "The blood of Jesus! The blood of Jesus!" At that instant, the man fell down weeping and apologizing. His evil spells had been canceled by the name and blood and authority of Jesus.

"He came to me to cast a spell on me or place a curse on me," Kaezad recalls. "I used the blood of Jesus, and there was no contest. The Lord won hands down on the enemy's turf."[1] That is the kind of authority over evil that we will witness in Mark 6.

Going Forth in Power

With this study, we move into the final division of the first half of Mark's gospel, the theme of which is the Servant who rules. Within part 1, these are four major divisions:

> The Authority of the Servant (Mark 1:1–39)
> The Servant's Knowledge of Our Humanity (Mark 1:40–3:6)
> The Problem of Popularity (Mark 3:7–6:6)
> "Who Is This?" (Mark 6:7–8:33)

The theme of this final section of part 1 comes from the words of the awestruck disciples after Jesus stilled the storm on the Sea of Galilee. As the storm subsided and a great calm settled on the lake, the disciples said to each other, "Who is this? Even the wind and the waves obey him!" (Mark 4:41). A little later, when Jesus went to Nazareth, His hometown, and was among the people He grew up with, they were similarly amazed at His teaching and said, "Where did this man get these things? What's this wisdom that has been given him, that he even does miracles! Isn't this the carpenter, Mary's son?" (Mark 6:2–3). They said this not because they were in awe of Jesus but because they were offended by Him. It is striking that the believing disciples and the unbelieving citizens of Nazareth asked the same question about Him: "Who is this?"

And in response to this growing question about Him, Jesus begins to teach the answer to His disciples. In the coming verses, we will see the disciples arrive at an answer to this all-important question, "Who is this?"

We begin with Mark's account of Jesus' commissioning of the Twelve on a special assignment.

> *Calling the Twelve to him, he sent them out two by two and gave them authority over evil spirits.*

> *These were his instructions: "Take nothing for the journey except a staff—no bread, no bag, no money in your belts. Wear sandals but not an extra tunic. Whenever you enter a house, stay there until you leave that town. And if any place will not welcome you or listen to you, shake the dust off your feet when you leave, as a testimony against them."*
>
> *They went out and preached that people should repent. They drove out many demons and anointed many sick people with oil and healed them.* (MARK 6:7–13)

Mark describes the commissioning of the twelve disciples for ministry. In this account, we find a number of key principles for Christian ministry today. The account of this event in Matthew 10 contains greater detail, but in this brief survey, Mark highlights three important facts.

First, Mark emphasizes the power the disciples exercised. Jesus sent them out and gave them authority over unclean spirits. I do not know how He did this, but our Lord imparted to them the same kind of authority that He possessed. They were able to exercise this authority over unclean spirits, even at a distance from Him. Much later, in the Upper Room, as He is about to leave them, Jesus tells them, "I will ask the Father, and he will give you another Counselor to be with you forever" (John 14:16). This implies that one Counselor was already there among them, and that Counselor was Jesus. He supplied the power and authority the disciples needed for this ministry.

Imagine what it must have been like for these disciples to test that power and authority for the first time. Confronted by a demonized person, fearful and uncertain, they would command the demon to depart in the name of Jesus, and the demon would obey. Matthew tells us that when they returned, the disciples were rejoicing that the demons were subject to them. They were amazed and praising God that, having gone forth in the name of Jesus, they had power over evil spirits by His name.

Second, Mark emphasizes the fact that this power was expressed in unity. The disciples did not go out individually. Our Lord never sent anyone to minister alone. He sent them out two by two. Matthew lists who went with whom. Andrew went with his brother, Peter. James went with his brother, John, and so on down the list. They went out two by two, in the unity of fellowship together, and the power and authority of Jesus was expressed through them.

I have always felt sorry for Simon the Zealot, because his partner was Judas Iscariot. It is amazing and sobering to remember that Judas too was given authority to cast out demons and heal the sick in Jesus' name. In fact, Matthew records that Jesus even gave His disciples authority to raise the dead. This ought to give us pause when we see power and authority exercised in Jesus' name. The exercise of such a ministry does not guarantee that the person is a genuine disciple, for Judas was, according to Jesus in John 6:70–71, "a devil" from the beginning.

Third, Mark emphasizes the fact that the disciples were given superiority over all forms of evil. They needed to fear nothing. He gave them authority even over one of the most potent enemies of humanity, unclean spirits. This implies that any Christian who goes out to minister in Jesus' name has His authority and need not be afraid to tackle anything. No entrenchment of evil is too difficult or dangerous for a Christian to confront. That is what this account suggests and what these disciples discovered when they went out.

Ministering in Complete Dependence

Next, notice how the disciples ministered in total dependence on God. Jesus made clear they were to go without any provision for their journey. He said, "Don't even go home and get ready. Go just as you are. Don't think about preparations. Take no food, or money to buy food. Trust God, and He will provide for you." Jesus deliberately sent them out this way to teach them lessons in faith, to teach them that God is able to provide and that everywhere they went, their needs would be met.

We also need to recognize, however, that this was in line with the general practice of that time. Hospitality was a cultural absolute in those Middle Eastern villages. Any stranger coming to town could expect to be received and cared for. So Jesus told them to expect hospitality. They had no Motel 6 in which to stay, but they knew that wherever they went, someone would "leave the light on" for them. We must read this account alongside Luke 22, where, near the close of Jesus' ministry, this exchange takes place between Jesus and His disciples:

> Then Jesus asked them, "When I sent you without purse, bag or sandals, did you lack anything?"
> "Nothing," they answered. He said to them, "But now if you have a purse, take it, and also a bag; and if you don't have a sword, sell your cloak and buy one." (LUKE 22:35–36)

This approach to the ministry of believers continued until the Lord reached the end of His ministry and the age of the Spirit was about to begin. Some people, having read this account of the first mission of the Twelve, hastily assume that we are to minister just as they did, without preparing adequately for our physical needs and our ministry needs. This shows how carelessly we sometimes read Scripture.

Our Lord makes it clear that this was a temporary provision, specifically for these men. This account does set forth an abiding and timeless principle: those who minister in the name of Jesus must do so in complete dependence on God. God must open the doors. God must plan the journey and make the opportunity and supply the needs, whatever preparation might be made in advance.

Note too that the disciples were not to go out as beggars. They were not to solicit hospitality or donations. They were going to give, not to get. They were clothed with authority, with power to bless and strengthen and heal. They were to share their God-given power and God-given peace whenever they came into a house. In the more detailed account in Matthew, Jesus tells the disciples that whenever they came to a house, they were to let their peace come on that household; they were to be a blessing to the family with whom they stayed. Furthermore, they were to exercise the power of their ministry in that household; they were to heal the sick and leave a blessing behind. So, as they went, they were giving far more than they got. This is another abiding principle of ministry. Ministry that is worthy of support is ministry that gives more than it gets.

Our Lord instructed His disciples that when they left a village or a town that did not receive them, they were to leave without regret, except to express a word of sorrow. This is what Jesus meant when He said they were to shake the dust from their feet wherever they were not received. It was not an act of vindictiveness but an expression of sorrow that the people of that place had refused God's blessing.

A Message of Repentance

Notice also the message the disciples preached. They went out preaching that people should repent. This was the message of John the Baptist. Repentance is the acknowledgment of wrong, the awareness that something is damaging your life, that you are doing things that are hurtful to yourself and to others. To admit that fact, without justifying or rationalizing it, is authentic repentance. When people responded with repentance to the preaching of the Twelve, the disciples ministered to them in the unique way recorded here: "They drove out many demons and anointed many sick people with oil and healed them."

I must confess that for years I used to read this account without really noticing that the disciples anointed with oil as part of their ministry. Jesus never anointed with oil, but the disciples did, evidently at His command. We can see a clear link between this passage and a passage where James, the brother of Jesus, writes, "Is any one of you sick? He should call the elders of the church to pray over him and anoint him with oil in the name of the Lord. And the prayer offered in faith will make the sick person well; the Lord will raise him up. If he has sinned, he will be forgiven" (James 5:14–15). This is evidently a reference to the apostles' practice of anointing with oil as they ministered from place to place.

As men and women came to the place of repentance, acknowledging their guilt and need, the disciples were empowered to administer forgiveness and healing in Jesus' name. People were to be forgiven and raised up when they repented. This casts a great deal of light on the passage in James. The disciples' ministry was a response to the problem of sin and evil in individuals.

We are likewise sent out by the same Lord, with authority to act against evil wherever we find it. At the same time, we must acknowledge our complete dependence on God to open the doors, provide the opportunities, and plan the strategies.

Ministry Shock Waves

The disciples go out and experience a powerful, effective ministry. In fact, their ministry is so influential that it sends shock waves into the halls of the Judean government, where Herod reigns as king. Mark writes:

> King Herod heard about this, for Jesus' name had become well known. Some were saying, "John the Baptist has been raised from the dead, and that is why miraculous powers are at work in him."
>
> Others said, "He is Elijah."
>
> And still others claimed, "He is a prophet, like one of the prophets of long ago."
>
> But when Herod heard this, he said, "John, the man I beheaded, has been raised from the dead!"
>
> (MARK 6:14–16)

Here we see two important effects of the ministry of the Twelve. First, the name of Jesus was magnified. The disciples were faithful to their commission. They did not magnify themselves; they magnified Jesus. The people did not ask, "Who are these men, that they do these mighty things?" They always asked, "Who is this Jesus, who has given them this power and authority?" Everywhere people were talking about Jesus and what He was doing through the Twelve. One of the great failures of the modern church is that we talk so much about what the church is doing instead of what the Lord is doing through us.

Second, the foundations of earthly power were shaken. Herod was frightened out of his wits. He thought that by killing John the Baptist, he had put out a smoldering fire. Suddenly that fire was blazing in dozens, scores, hundreds of new places. This is how God works. When someone raises opposition to the gospel and squelches it in one place, it is like pouring water on burning oil. It doesn't extinguish the fire; it splashes the fire all around. When

Herod realized what he had done, he was frightened, and well he should have been.

It is remarkable that Herod thought that John the Baptist was raised from the dead and appearing in all these various places. The Bible tells us that John did no miracles while he was alive. Yet when Herod hears of the miracles of Jesus, he immediately associates them with a risen John the Baptist. This is all the more amazing in that Herod belonged to the party of the Sadducees, who were rationalists and antisupernaturalists. They did not believe in resurrection. But a guilty conscience is a powerful thing. It can turn a person's worldview upside down. As Shakespeare observed, "Conscience doth make cowards of us all."

Mark then gives us a flashback to the death of John the Baptist, which occurred just before the disciples were sent out.

> For Herod himself had given orders to have John arrested, and he had him bound and put in prison. He did this because of Herodias, his brother Philip's wife, whom he had married. For John had been saying to Herod, "It is not lawful for you to have your brother's wife." (MARK 6:17–18)

The marital entanglements of this family of Herods are incredible. They started with Herod the Great, who married five different wives and had children by each woman. Then the progeny began to marry each other and each other's progeny. Cousins were marrying, and this Herod—Herod Antipas—married his niece, Herodias, who had been the wife of his half-brother Philip. To further complicate the story, there was another half-brother also named Philip.

But I am not going to try to sort it all out for you. It is enough to recognize that this was a public scandal. And John the Baptist had publicly rebuked the king for seducing his brother's wife and marrying her. Herod did not seem to be greatly offended by John's rebuke, but Herodias was. She demanded John's arrest and, later, his murder. Mark writes:

> *So Herodias nursed a grudge against John and wanted to kill him. But she was not able to, because Herod feared John and protected him, knowing him to be a righteous and holy man. When Herod heard John, he was greatly puzzled; yet he liked to listen to him.*
>
> *Finally the opportune time came. On his birthday Herod gave a banquet for his high officials and military commanders and the leading men of Galilee. When the daughter of Herodias came in and danced, she pleased Herod and his dinner guests.*
>
> *The king said to the girl, "Ask me for anything you want, and I'll give it to you." And he promised her with an oath, "Whatever you ask I will give you, up to half my kingdom."*
>
> *She went out and said to her mother, "What shall I ask for?"*
>
> *"The head of John the Baptist," she answered.*
>
> *At once the girl hurried in to the king with the request: "I want you to give me right now the head of John the Baptist on a platter."*
>
> *The king was greatly distressed, but because of his oaths and his dinner guests, he did not want to refuse her. So he immediately sent an executioner with orders to bring John's head. The man went, beheaded John in the prison, and brought back his head on a platter. He presented it to the girl, and she gave it to her mother. On hearing of this, John's disciples came and took his body and laid it in a tomb.* (MARK 6:19–29)

This is a grisly story of a woman's hate and a man's weakness. Herodias was a bitter woman who hated John because of his exposure of her evil, so she constantly worked to destroy him. But Herod listened to John and seemed to like him. All of this took place in that forbidding castle called Machaerus, on the east side of the Dead Sea, the ruins of which are still there. You can visit the dungeons and see where the chains were fastened to the walls, and where John the Baptist was undoubtedly held prisoner. In that remote fortress, Herod gave his banquet, watched Salome dance, and grievously and reluctantly granted her gruesome request. In that castle, the weakness of Herod's character was revealed for all to see.

Mark has given us this account because it explains why Jesus sent out the twelve disciples. When John was first arrested, Jesus began His ministry in Galilee. After John was beheaded, Jesus sent out the Twelve to continue John's ministry. They are sent out with the same message John preached: the message of repentance. But Jesus added a new dimension to their ministry that John's ministry did not have: the authority to cast out demons and power to heal the physically, emotionally, and spiritually sick; the ability to heal those afflicted by guilt and sin.

The Lord was teaching His disciples the full breadth and depth of the gospel. They didn't understand who He was or what He had come to do, which was to die for the sins of the human race. They knew only that God was at work in Israel and that people had to acknowledge their sinfulness and their need. Then God would begin to work in their lives. This is where the gospel starts—with repentance. And little by little, these other elements are added as we go along. So the Twelve continued the ministry of John, but they also ministered in new ways beyond what John had been able to accomplish.

Fed by a Miracle

Now we come to the final two incidents of this section, which show what follows when the Twelve return from their mission. The first incident is the feeding of the five thousand, and we will soon see how this incident fits into the pattern of events. But first let us listen to the report of the Twelve on their return.

> *The apostles gathered around Jesus and reported to him all they had done and taught. Then, because so many people were coming and going that they did not even have a chance to eat, he said to them, "Come with me by yourselves to a quiet place and get some rest."* (MARK 6:30–31)

Jesus recognized this as a period of danger for His disciples. They needed rest, and He made provision for it. They needed time to think through what had happened. Matthew's and Luke's accounts of this return show that the disciples were excited by their ministry. They were amazed and encouraged by the results they had seen, and they came back like boys let out of school, eager to report to Jesus everything that had happened. They were so exuberant that Jesus had to caution them, "However, do not rejoice that the spirits submit to you, but rejoice that your names are written in heaven" (Luke 10:20). He could see that they were in danger of being caught up with spiritual pride, and He wanted to protect them from it.

This is the first time that the Twelve are called apostles. They had been disciples up to now, but now they had been sent out, and that is what an apostle is—one who is sent out. They had been given a ministry of their own.

An important principle of teaching and mentoring is embedded in this passage. Many churches, ministry schools, and ministry programs operate on the belief that people must be thoroughly trained before they can be put to work. You have to stuff their heads full of knowledge and make sure they can answer all the great theological questions before they can be useful to God. Only when they have a degree from a seminary or ministry school can they be ready to work for God.

That was not our Lord's way. He sent out ignorant men who did not even begin to grasp the fullness of the message they were preaching. They hardly knew what they were doing. But Jesus sent them out and gave them power to act, and He expected them to learn as they went. In my church ministry, I have seen this to be true. You should not wait until you know it all before you act. Rather, act on the little you know, and learn more as you go along. Christian ministry is on-the-job training.

Of course, early successes can create swelled heads, especially among immature followers. This is why Jesus took His disciples away to a lonely place, so that He could minister to them and teach them. But He had some difficulty along the way.

So they went away by themselves in a boat to a solitary place. But many who saw them leaving recognized them and ran on foot from all the towns and got there ahead of them. When Jesus landed and saw a large crowd, he had compassion on them, because they were like sheep without a shepherd. So he began teaching them many things. (MARK 6:32–34)

How would you have reacted in Jesus' place? Here they were, trying to get away from the crowd, trying to escape the pressure and crush of the masses, trying to find a few moments of peace and rest. So they went across the lake, only to find that the crowds were already waiting for them there. I think I would have lost my temper and said, "Can't you leave us alone for one moment? Don't you have any concern for us and our needs?"

But notice how Jesus handled the situation. See the heart of a shepherd at work. Remember, it was He who said, "Blessed are those who hunger and thirst for righteousness, for they will be filled" (Matthew 5:6). And even though these crowds were intrusive and bothersome, these people were so hungry for deliverance that they willingly ran ten miles by foot around the northern end of the lake to meet Him when He arrived. They hungered and thirsted for the truth He came to bring them. So, wearily but without a word of rebuke, Jesus began to teach them.

I do not know what He taught. Perhaps we have something of it in John's account, where Jesus taught about the bread from heaven. Or perhaps He reprised some of His thoughts from the Sermon on the Mount. Whatever He taught, Mark tells us He did a wonderful, amazing thing.

> By this time it was late in the day, so his disciples came to him. "This is a remote place," they said, "and it's already very late. Send the people away so they can go to the surrounding countryside and villages and buy themselves something to eat."
>
> But he answered, "You give them something to eat."
>
> They said to him, "That would take eight months of a man's wages! Are we to go and spend that much on bread and give it to them to eat?"
>
> "How many loaves do you have?" he asked. "Go and see."
>
> When they found out, they said, "Five—and two fish."
>
> Then Jesus directed them to have all the people sit down in groups on the green grass. So they sat down in groups of hundreds and fifties. (MARK 6:35–40)

This is a vivid description. It undoubtedly reflects Peter's memory of the event, which he related to Mark. This is the only miracle, by the way, that is recorded in all four gospels. Peter's memory of this event, as recounted by Mark, was so vivid that he even remembered the green grass growing all over the hills in the month of April, when this took place.

There is an interesting visual picture here that the English translation doesn't capture. The word translated "groups" is the word used for rows of vegetables in a garden. Mark describes the people sitting down on the green grass, giving the appearance of rows of vegetables in a vast vegetable garden. In his mind's eye, Peter could still see the clusters of people, sitting on the beautiful green hillside, lined up like vegetables in rows, waiting for Jesus to speak. Mark continues the account:

> *Taking the five loaves and the two fish and looking up to heaven, he gave thanks and broke the loaves. Then he gave them to his disciples to set before the people. He also divided the two fish among them all. They all ate and were satisfied, and the disciples picked up twelve basketfuls of broken pieces of bread and fish. The number of the men who had eaten was five thousand.* (MARK 6:41–44)

We should draw from this miracle three important implications. First, this was a deliberate action by our Lord. These people were not so hungry that He had to feed them. Later on, when He fed the four thousand, they had been without food for three days. But here it is questionable that they had been without food for even one day. They had run around the lake and were very tired, perhaps, but not starving. Nevertheless He chose to feed them.

Second, Jesus performed this miracle in order to teach His disciples. This was primarily for their benefit. What He did was designed to remind them of the feeding of the multitudes of Israel in the wilderness, when the manna came down from heaven. He was drawing a deliberate picture of who He was for these disciples. This is why John records that He said to them, "I am the bread that came down from heaven" (John 6:41). The disciples were expected to see in this miracle a symbol of the one they were following. But they seemed to miss the point.

Third, this event was related to God's ministry to Israel. Mark says, "The disciples picked up twelve basketfuls of broken pieces of bread and fish." As we have seen, the number twelve is usually symbolic of God's people, and particularly of the twelve tribes of Israel. Jesus said He chose twelve disciples so that they might sit on twelve thrones judging the twelve tribes of Israel. In the previous section we saw a dying girl who was twelve years old and a woman who had an issue of blood for twelve years. Now twelve baskets of food are taken up. This is a reminder to the disciples that Jesus is the promised one, the great provider who was foretold as coming to Israel.

An F on the Exam

Yet, even after Jesus gave the disciples this vivid object lesson, their eyes were shut. So another, even more vivid object lesson immediately follows.

> *Immediately Jesus made his disciples get into the boat and go on ahead of him to Bethsaida, while he dismissed the crowd. After leaving them, he went up on a mountainside to pray.*
>
> *When evening came, the boat was in the middle of the lake, and he was alone on land. He saw the disciples straining*

at the oars, because the wind was against them. About the
fourth watch of the night he went out to them, walking on
the lake. He was about to pass by them, but when they saw
him walking on the lake, they thought he was a ghost. They
cried out, because they all saw him and were terrified.

Immediately he spoke to them and said, "Take courage!
It is I. Don't be afraid." Then he climbed into the boat with
them, and the wind died down. They were completely
amazed, for they had not understood about the loaves; their
hearts were hardened. (MARK 6:45–52)

It appears that this miracle is a test or exam given to the disciples after the feeding of the five thousand. Our Lord had sent
them out and given them power. They saw their ministry con-
firmed and authenticated by the hand of God working through
them. They had come back excited and buoyant over all they had
seen and done. They had now been taught that Jesus was the one
who was coming to fulfill the expectation of Israel's promised
Messiah.

Yet they still missed the central truth of what Jesus was trying to tell them about Himself.

So He gave them an examination, a test, to see if they were
starting to understand. He sent them out into a storm. They had
been in such a storm once before, but this time it is different.
Before He was in the boat with them, sleeping in the back. This
time He deliberately sent them out by themselves while He went
up into the hills to pray.

And here we see a perfect metaphor for the storms of our
lives. Truly the stormy times of life seem to consist of two elements: overwhelming circumstances of trouble or opposition and
the seeming absence of the Lord. Of course, Jesus is never truly

absent. He is always interceding on our behalf, just as He was on the hillside, praying for His disciples.

After the storm has blown for several hours and the disciples are in deep distress, Jesus comes to them walking on the water. When they see Him, they are terrified, thinking He is a ghost. He has to reassure them, "It is I. Don't be afraid." Then Jesus walks up and climbs into the boat. Mark records that they were "amazed." An equally appropriate word might be "flabbergasted," for this word suggests the grade the disciples earned on their exam: a big red F. They got an F for failure, for fear, for flabbergasted.

Once again the disciples' eyes were opened to the question "Who is this?" They were given a powerful object lesson in faith, and this experience served to open the door for some of our Lord's greatest teaching about who He was and why He came.

Who is this? Who is this who comes walking on the water? Who sends storms into our lives to test us? Who makes provision for our needs and then tests us on our reliance on Him? Who always makes intercession for us, even when He seems to be absent and remote?

Jesus the Lord.

twelve

When Rite Is Wrong

➤ **Mark 6:53–7:30**

One of the longest-running shows in Broadway history is *Fiddler on the Roof,* the story of a Russian-Jewish milk peddler named Tevye, his wife, Golde, and their five daughters, who break tradition by choosing their husbands. The opening song, "Tradition," sets the tone for this timeless musical play, based on the stories of Sholem Aleichem. The title of the play is explained early on when Tevye says, "Without our traditions, our lives would be as shaky as a fiddler on the roof!"

The play rings with truth—the truth that the Jewish community has been built on and governed by long-standing, unbreakable traditions. The unspoken thesis of the play is that hidebound, inflexible adherence to tradition is destructive, bringing grief and hardship into human lives. That is also the theme of this passage. Mark shows the stark contrast between the ministry of Jesus, who reaches out to men and women with God's healing love, and the Pharisees, who, armed with tradition, seek to shut down the ministry of God's love.

Thomas Dickson, one of the great preachers of the nineteenth century, once said, "Tradition was the most constant, the most persistent, the most dogged, the most utterly devilish opposition the Master encountered. It openly attacked him on every hand and silently repulsed his teaching." That is what we will see in this passage.

Isaiah's Words Fulfilled

We begin with the closing words of Mark 6, where Mark describes for us once again the healing ministry of our Lord:

> *When they had crossed over, they landed at Gennesaret and anchored there. As soon as they got out of the boat, people recognized Jesus. They ran throughout that whole region and carried the sick on mats to wherever they heard he was. And wherever he went—into villages, towns or country-side—they placed the sick in the marketplaces. They begged him to let them touch even the edge of his cloak, and all who touched him were healed.* (MARK 6:53–56)

This is a powerful illustration of the far-reaching ministry of Jesus. Obviously the story of the woman with the issue of blood has spread. People have heard that she was healed by touching the hem of Jesus' garment, and now many people bring the sick and demonized for one touch of that now-famous hem. The result, says Mark, is that "all who touched him were healed." This is a wonderful fulfillment of this majestic passage in Isaiah:

> *Then will the eyes of the blind be opened*
> *and the ears of the deaf unstopped.*
> *Then will the lame leap like a deer,*
> *and the mute tongue shout for joy.* (ISAIAH 35:5–6)

The Power of Tradition

From this beautiful scene, Mark immediately moves to the story of opposition from a delegation of Pharisees and scribes.

> *The Pharisees and some of the teachers of the law who had come from Jerusalem gathered around Jesus and saw some of his disciples eating food with hands that were "unclean," that is, unwashed. (The Pharisees and all the Jews do not eat unless they give their hands a ceremonial washing, holding to the tradition of the elders. When they come from the marketplace they do not eat unless they wash. And they observe many other traditions, such as the washing of cups, pitchers and kettles.)* (MARK 7:1–4)

This section introduces us to the power of tradition. In this opening paragraph of Mark 7, we see something of the effect of tradition on our lives. Not only was this true of the Hebrew culture in that day; it is also true of our Christian culture. Some of us attend church because it is traditional to do so. We expect certain forms of liturgy, certain hymns, certain rites, and certain religious practices in our worship service because it is traditional to do it that way. Tradition is the power of the past reaching into the present to shape our future. We all observe and obey some traditions at one time or another.

Is tradition a good thing or a bad thing? From the example and teaching of Jesus, we will see that it can be good or bad, depending on how we observe it.

Notice that the delegation from Jerusalem came to entrap Jesus. Word of this fast-spreading popular movement had reached Jerusalem, and the chief priests and rulers of the Jews were troubled by it. They knew that if they could show that Jesus had violated or snubbed the popularly accepted traditions of Judaism, they could turn the crowd against Him. This indicates how strongly these traditions were held.

The tradition the Pharisees chose had to do with the washing of hands. The religious leaders observed Jesus and the disciples, and they saw that some of them did not wash their hands in the prescribed way before they ate. This does not mean the disciples were dirty or had hygiene problems. I'm sure they did wash their hands before they ate. What bothered the Pharisees was that they did not wash in the traditional, ceremonial way.

Among the Jews of that time, you could have washed your hands with the finest of soaps and scrubbed like a doctor preparing for surgery. But if you did not wash according to the ancient religious rites and traditions, then you were just as ceremonially unclean as if you had not washed.

In the Revised Standard Version a margin note states that one word in verse 3, the phrase "wash their hands," "is of uncertain meaning and is not translated." It is the word for "fist." The translators evidently had difficulty understanding how this word fit into the context.

But scholars say that it was a ceremonial tradition among the Jews to wash in a specific way. The hands had to be held out, palms up, hands cupped slightly, and water poured over them. Then the fist of one hand was used to scrub the other, and then the other fist would scrub the first hand. This is why the fist is mentioned here. Finally the hands again were held out, with palms down, and water was poured over them a second time to cleanse away the dirty water. Only then would a person's hands be ceremonially clean. They might not be hygienically clean, but they would be ceremonially clean. Tradition would be satisfied.

So strongly was this tradition ingrained th.
was imprisoned by the Romans, he used the
brought to him in his solitary dungeon cell to wash
this way. He would die of thirst before he would allow
be ceremonially unclean.

Were the traditions wrong? No. The traditions had beg.
the right way and for the right reasons. They began as an atten.
to apply the law of God. The book of Leviticus did require that
certain ablutions, certain washings, be performed as a way of
teaching the people how to handle sin. That was the intent of the
law. But as these requirements were applied to various situations,
human rules accumulated to describe the ceremonially proper
way to do things. Over time, the priests interpreted and reinter-
preted these rules; more rules were added. Gradually, over the
years and centuries, a tremendous mass of tradition accumulated
that demanded inflexible obedience and scrupulous observance
of even the most minor details. Instead of God's law, the people
had hundreds and hundreds of human laws and rules and traditions to obey. The original, holy purpose of the law was forgotten.
All that mattered was tradition.

Before we judge the ancient Jews too harshly for becoming
rigid and tradition-bound, we should realize that the same thing
has happened in the church of Jesus Christ. Again and again,
down through the ages, the church has needed reformation and
rescue from the enslavement of rigid tradition.

The church was never intended to be tradition-bound. In the
book of Acts we see that the Holy Spirit moved with amazing freedom and spontaneity among the people of God. The Lord never
worked the same way twice in the book of Acts. It is beautiful to
see the newness and creativity of the Spirit in Acts. We cannot
deduce any permanent rites or static rituals for the church from

because God is constantly doing a new and work.

churches have done with the book of Acts what the vs did with the law of Moses. They settled on this or that form as the right way to do things for all time. added rules and interpretations, liturgies and orders of serv- . Deeds that the Spirit once wrote in water have now become chiseled in stone. Freedom has turned to bondage. What was once done with joy is now done out of obligation. We no longer keep traditions; tradition keeps us. The mindset that confronts our Lord in this passage is tragically alive and well in the church today.

Tradition Produces Hypocrites

In the next section, we read the words of Jesus with regard to tradition, and we begin to see how a tradition begins as a living heritage and ends up as a dead formality.

> So the Pharisees and teachers of the law asked Jesus, "Why don't your disciples live according to the tradition of the elders instead of eating their food with 'unclean' hands?"
> He replied, "Isaiah was right when he prophesied about you hypocrites; as it is written:
>
> "'These people honor me with their lips,
>   but their hearts are far from me.
> They worship me in vain;
>   their teachings are but rules taught by men.'"
>   (MARK 7:5–7)

These insightful words of Jesus cut to the heart of the issue. When the Pharisees ask Him, "Why do your disciples not observe the traditions?" Jesus points out to them the effect that tradition has on their lives: it produces hypocrites. "Isaiah was right when he prophesied about you hypocrites," He says.

I am amazed at Jesus' bluntness! Matthew's account tells us that the disciples said to Him afterward, "Do you know the Pharisees were offended when they heard this?" (Matthew 15:12).

But notice what Jesus is doing. He is pointing out the result of traditional worship, and He uses the words of the prophet Isaiah to show us what it is like. There are two kinds of hypocrisy, according to Isaiah: right words but wrong attitudes and worldly philosophies disguised as religious devotion. Let's look at each of these forms of hypocrisy.

First Form of Hypocrisy: *Right Words, Wrong Attitudes*

With this kind of hypocrisy, everything outward is right, but inwardly the mind and heart are wrong. Isaiah put it this way: "These people honor me with their lips, but their hearts are far from me." That, Jesus says, is hypocrisy: to look as if you are doing something religious and worshipful toward God but to have a totally different attitude inside.

During the youth revolt and counterculture movement of the 1960s, many of us in the church were puzzled and offended when young people would say to us, "We don't want to have anything to do with the church because churches are full of hypocrites." Some of us could not understand what they meant. We knew there might be some hypocrites in some churches, but not in our churches, and not us. We are sincere, Bible-believing Christians in a strong, evangelical church.

But what these rebellious young people were saying to us was this: "You use great words, wonderful words, God words, but you don't mean them. You talk about love, but you don't love. You talk about forgiveness, but you don't forgive. You talk about acceptance, but you don't accept." And they were right.

That is what tradition does to us. It externalizes religion, makes it outward instead of inward. As long as we are fulfilling the outward form of religion, we think we are acceptable before God. In time, tradition causes people to focus on the form and forget the substance. People think that their faith is all about right words, and they forget that their attitudes are wrong, their hearts are far from God. As a result, we evangelical Christians easily fall prey to the sins of arrogance and self-righteousness. We think that because we do things in the right way, and say the right words, and believe the right doctrines, we are right with God, when nothing could be further from the truth.

I have a Christian friend, a businessman, who once sent me a perceptive article he had written on the danger of self-righteousness in the church. The article is called "Don't Take Me to the Hospital, Please!" I will paraphrase and condense it for you.

A man is in the street, bleeding and broken, the victim of a hit-and-run accident. He needs medical help, but when the ambulance arrives, he tells the paramedics, "Please don't take me to the hospital!" The surprised paramedics ask him why he doesn't want to be hospitalized.

"Because," the man answers, "I'm on the hospital staff. It would be embarrassing to have the people at the hospital see me like this. They've never seen me bleeding and dirty. What would they think if they saw me in this condition?"

"But," the paramedics argue, "the hospital is for injured people like you! You must let us take you to the hospital!"

"No, you don't understand!" the man pleads. "I took a pedestrian safety course, and the instructor would criticize me for getting hit."

"But who cares what the instructor thinks? You're bleeding, you may have internal injuries, and you may die without medical attention!"

"But the admissions clerk at the hospital would be upset."

"Why?"

"I don't have my Blue Cross card on me! She's a real stickler for accurate information."

"We can get all that information later. Right now, you need to go to the hospital!"

"But look at me! I'm a mess! My clothes all torn and bloody, and my hair is out of place! I can't let anyone at the hospital see me like this! Just move me over into the gutter and let me crawl back home."

I know what you're thinking: what a ridiculous attitude!

Yet this attitude is commonplace in the church. On one occasion, I asked a group of active, involved Christians in my church if they would go to church on Sunday after getting caught in a scandalous sin. Without exception, they said, "I sure wouldn't go to church! Everyone would see me! Everyone would know! What would they think of me?" In other words, they would feel ostracized and condemned by the people who talk about grace, love, and forgiveness. It seems there's no room in the church for a dirty saint.

As I talked with this group of Christians, one of them suggested that if we are caught in an unacceptable sin, we are better off going to a pool hall than to church. At a pool hall, you'll find sympathy and understanding. Nobody will judge you there. Instead, someone will say, "Hey, buddy, this isn't the end of the world. I've been where you are, and I got through it." Another would say, "You need a good lawyer, pal? Let me recommend a guy who helped me." And another would say, "You know, you seem like one of us now. You're okay."

The question that should trouble us in the church is this: Where should real love and understanding live? In a pool hall? Or in the church of Jesus Christ, who died for sinners?

Our Lord had a plan when He founded His church. His plan was that the church would be a hospital for sinners. When people are reeling and wounded after being caught in some terrible sin, the first words on their lips should be, "Get me to the church—fast!" The reason people don't look at the church that way is obvious. The church *is* full of hypocrites. To paraphrase Pogo, we have met the hypocrites, and they are us.

We talk about love, but we think and act in judgment and condemnation. We have the right words but the wrong attitudes. That is what our Lord is warning us about.

Second Form of Hypocrisy: *Worldly Philosophies Disguised as Religion*

Isaiah describes the second form of hypocrisy: "They worship me in vain; their teachings are but rules taught by men." This refers to outwardly religious actions that cloak and disguise worldly philosophies. This form of hypocrisy is widespread in the church. It is the idea that if we take the principles and the precepts by which the world operates and dress them up with Scripture passages, then we are worshiping God. That is how the church has become infected with so many false beliefs and doctrines. Many of these false beliefs invade the church quietly and stealthily. Before we know it, tendrils of New Age philosophy, Eastern mysticism, Hollywood immorality, dog-eat-dog business ethics, secular psychology and psychiatry, social Darwinism, and other non-Christian thought forms have become woven into our thinking. Like weeds in a garden, false ideas spring up among us and begin to choke out the truth of God's Word. Jesus says that is hypocrisy.

Perhaps we are beginning to look at our churches and our lives with new eyes. It is easy to say, "Those foolish Pharisees! They had the truth of the Old Testament, yet they infected it with human rules and similar nonsense. They corrupted God's truth with human traditions." But if we are honest, we must look at the many ways we in the Christian church have done the same thing.

We have corrupted the gospel of Jesus Christ with human worldly philosophies and ideas. We have rationalized our worldliness by twisting bits and pieces of Scripture to fit our worldly ideas. We have traded God's truth for human traditions. We have become hypocrites, and we are no less foolish than the Pharisees we are so quick to condemn.

The Origin of Sin and Hypocrisy

Look at what our Lord says next. He has shown us the danger of tradition, which leads to hypocrisy. Now He shows where hypocrisy leads.

> *"You have let go of the commands of God and are holding on to the traditions of men."*
>
> *And he said to them: "You have a fine way of setting aside the commands of God in order to observe your own traditions! For Moses said, 'Honor your father and your mother,' and, 'Anyone who curses his father or mother must be put to death.' But you say that if a man says to his father or mother: 'Whatever help you might otherwise have received from me is Corban' (that is, a gift devoted to God), then you no longer let him do anything for his father or mother. Thus you nullify the word of God by your tradition that you have handed down. And you do many things like that."* (MARK 7:8–13)

With those incisive words, our Lord traces for us what happens when tradition begins to gain sway. First, it begins with abandoning the commands of God. Traditions arise when we try to find a substitute to give God instead of the authentic worship He wants.

Two Christian businessmen once met for lunch. One said, "Everything in my life is going wrong. I'm about to lose my business. My personal life is falling apart. I don't understand why, because for years I've faithfully given money to God. I tithe regularly, yet everything is falling apart." The other man replied, "Did you ever stop to think that what God wants is not your money but you?" And that is precisely the question the failing businessman needed to confront. He had lost sight of the authentic worship God truly wanted from him. That is where hypocrisy begins—with the abandonment of God's commands.

The second step, as our Lord indicates, is that we begin to deny God and injure other people. He illustrates it with an example about fathers and mothers. The law says, "Honor your father and your mother, so that you may live long in the land the LORD your God is giving you" (Exodus 20:12). That means more than being courteous to parents; it means taking care of them, especially as they grow older.

The Jewish leaders had worked out a neat rationale for abandoning parents. Jesus congratulated them (ironically, of course) for the cleverness with which they did this. They took the money that should have been spent on their parents, and they said, "This is a gift to God." Once the money was declared to be dedicated to God, these people were free to use it themselves. Their parents could not touch it because it was dedicated to God. So they had come up with a religious-sounding way to violate God's law about honoring parents. Jesus exposed this hypocrisy for what it was.

But our Lord didn't stop there. He proceeded to expose for us the true source of good and evil.

> *Again Jesus called the crowd to him and said, "Listen to me, everyone, and understand this. Nothing outside a man can make him 'unclean' by going into him. Rather, it is what comes out of a man that makes him 'unclean.'"*
>
> *After he had left the crowd and entered the house, his disciples asked him about this parable. "Are you so dull?" he asked. "Don't you see that nothing that enters a man from the outside can make him 'unclean'? For it doesn't go into his heart but into his stomach, and then out of his body." (In saying this, Jesus declared all foods "clean.")*
>
> *He went on: "What comes out of a man is what makes him 'unclean.' For from within, out of men's hearts, come evil thoughts, sexual immorality, theft, murder, adultery, greed, malice, deceit, lewdness, envy, slander, arrogance and folly. All these evils come from inside and make a man 'unclean.'"*
>
> (MARK 7:14–23)

Jesus addressed not just the Pharisees but also the entire crowd. He said nothing is inherently wrong with traditions, rites, and customs, nor are they inherently good. What you do outwardly with regard to traditions is neither bad nor good. Good or evil is determined by the intentions of the heart. The same practice can be wholesome and healthy if your heart is right toward God, and it can be useless and defiled if your heart toward God is evil, selfish, and rebellious. In that statement, Jesus put His finger on the source of evil within us.

Traditions and rites do not justify us, nor do they condemn us. Those who observe traditions and rites have no justification for feeling self-righteous. Those who do not observe traditions and rites have no right to look down on those who do. Good and evil proceed from the intentions, the will, the thoughts, the innermost being of a person.

Understanding this truth will deliver us from becoming self-righteous snobs. And let us be clear: there are snobs on both sides of this issue. Some Christians practice traditional, formal, liturgical worship, and they look down their noses at many of the newer, nontraditional forms of church worship. "Where are the pastors' robes?" they ask. "And where is the ornate, carved pulpit? Where are the chancel choir, the traditional hymns, the recited creeds and doxologies, the stained glass and Gothic architecture? That's not a true church. They have rejected all the traditions that make a church great!"

But other Christian snobs say, "Look at those poor, old-fashioned, tradition-bound souls! Haven't they heard of Christian freedom? Why are they still stuck in the nineteenth century? That's not a true church. They are trapped and enslaved by all the meaningless traditions that have kept the church in chains for centuries!" Christian snobbery cuts both ways.

What our Lord has outlined is a danger for every Christian, including you and me. It does no good to comb through this list and say, "Well, that's not me," and "I don't do that." Jesus tells us, "If you are guilty of one of these sins, you are guilty, period."

A Christian man once had a conversation with a saintly Christian woman. She startled the man by saying, "There is not one sin of which I am incapable. I could be a prostitute, I could be a murderess, I could be a thief." The man assumed that the saintly woman was speaking out of a deep sense of humility, and he congratulated her for it. But she rebuked him for that. "You don't believe I meant what I just said, but I assure you I *do* mean it—explicitly and literally. I am capable of those sins and more! I *need* this awareness of my capacity for sin. If I ever meet a person who has committed a sin, and I can say, 'I'm not capable of doing what he or she did,' then I cannot love that person. The same sinfulness that others are capable of also lurks in me. It may express itself in other ways, but it is there. Until I fully and absolutely believe that, I am nothing but a proud, self-righteous, arrogant woman."

That is a blunt restatement of what our Lord is telling us. There is no difference between sinners. We are all alike. Only the redemptive process of God frees us from the sin that comes from within. Evil pervades the human heart, and this is what defiles us in the sight of God. Nothing we do outwardly—no rite, ceremony, or observance—makes us any better or worse in God's eyes. He looks on the heart.

Children and Dogs

Mark makes an immediate connection between Jesus' teaching about tradition and another incident. It may seem at first as though Mark has changed the subject, but he has not. Mark writes:

> *Jesus left that place and went to the vicinity of Tyre. He entered a house and did not want anyone to know it; yet he could not keep his presence secret. In fact, as soon as she heard about him, a woman whose little daughter was possessed by an evil spirit came and fell at his feet. The woman was a Greek, born in Syrian Phoenicia. She begged Jesus to drive the demon out of her daughter.*
>
> *"First let the children eat all they want," he told her, "for it is not right to take the children's bread and toss it to their dogs."*

> *"Yes, Lord,"* she replied, *"but even the dogs under the*
> *table eat the children's crumbs."*
> *Then he told her, "For such a reply, you may go; the*
> *demon has left your daughter."*
> *She went home and found her child lying on the bed, and*
> *the demon gone.* (MARK 7:24–30)

This passage is disturbing for many people, and it is not hard to see why. Two questions are frequently asked about this incident.

First, why does Jesus treat this woman so harshly? Matthew's account of this same incident makes Him seem even ruder to her; he says that when she first asked Him to heal her daughter, He would not answer her. Many people have wondered why. I think the answer is in Matthew's account, where we are told that she first addressed Him in this way: "Lord, Son of David, have mercy on me! My daughter is suffering terribly from demon-possession" (Matthew 15:22). "Son of David" is a Jewish term for the Jewish Messiah. She was coming to Him in full awareness of the fact that He was a Jew and she was a Gentile. That is why He said to her, "The children first must be fed," because it was God's program that the gospel go to the Jews first and then to the Gentiles.

Jesus never intended for the Gentiles to be excluded from the gospel. But there was an order to be followed. The gospel should go to the Jews first, then to the Gentiles. And when this woman came on that basis, invoking all the power of Jewish tradition, he said to her, "It is not right to take the children's bread and throw it to the dogs." (He used a diminutive form, indicating pet dogs, not mangy street dogs.)

In other words, "It is not right to give God's blessing to the Gentiles before it has been offered to the Jews. You will have to wait until the time comes, until the gospel goes out to the Gentiles. Then I can heal your daughter. By coming on this basis, you have imposed limits on God. You have placed yourself in the position of a pet dog rather than a child of the family. Until that barrier is removed, I cannot give you what you ask."

But then the story takes a refreshing turn. The woman is in such agony for her child that she refuses to take no for an answer. She continues to press her case. "Yes, Lord," she says, agreeing with His assessment of herself as a Gentile pet dog rather than a true child of Israel. She says, "I know that's right. The children ought to eat first, and then the dogs. But even the dogs eat the crumbs that fall from the children's table." Then she said, as Matthew records in his gospel, "Lord, help me!"

Do you see what has happened? The woman began by appealing to tradition, to Jesus' position as the promised Messiah of Israel, and on that basis, He slammed the door in her face. But she persisted, approaching Him again not according to tradition but according to her desperate need. She was a loving mother with a suffering child, and her plea became a simple one: "Lord, help me." At that moment, our Lord's answer was immediate and caring: "For such a reply, you may go; the demon has left your daughter."

Jesus was not being cruel. He was teaching this woman what she needed to know about the love of God and the worthlessness of tradition. Although Jesus ignored her fine words addressed to the Jewish tradition, He responded to her needy plea.

The second question people ask about this passage is why Jesus went into Tyre and Sidon. These were two Gentile cities, populated by Canaanites. The woman in the story was a Canaanite woman of Greek extraction, born in Syrian Phoenicia. Yet, as soon as Jesus finished teaching on tradition, where did He immediately go? To the Gentile cities of Tyre and Sidon. Why? The obvious answer is that, like so many other things He has done in this section of Mark, He is teaching important lessons to His disciples. What is He teaching them by going to these Gentile cities? He is illustrating in terms of peoples and racial groups what He had just said in terms of food.

The Pharisees had said it is a sin to eat unclean foods with unclean hands. Jesus countered by saying that all foods are clean, and next He made the point that all people are clean, in the sense of being accepted by God. There are no distinctions among foods, as being defiling or undefiling; and there are no distinctions among people, as being defiled or undefiled by reason of race. So Jesus led the disciples to a Gentile city, in order that their tradition-bound Jewish outlook might be challenged, so that they could begin to see non-Jewish people as God sees them.

By this incident, Mark wants us to learn that tradition has a tendency to build barriers between God and us. But faith cuts across tradition like a hot knife cuts through butter. It cuts straight to the heart of God. When we come to God in simple faith, without rite or ritual or prescribed words but merely with a needy, open heart, God's answer is instant. And His healing is immediate and complete.

thirteen

"Do You Still Not Understand?"

➤ **Mark 7:31–8:21**

When I was a boy, I felt that the worst thing that could happen would be to become blind. I felt sorry for blind people and was fearful that some accident would take my sight. But in recent years, I have concluded that it would be much worse to be unable to hear and speak than to be unable to see. When you are unable to hear and speak, you are shut off from society even more completely than if you are blind.

In the closing section of Mark 7, we encounter a man whose world is silent, whose lips are silent. He cannot hear what anyone says to him. He cannot ask questions. He cannot receive answers. He lives in a world of silence, isolated from the people around him, who pass him by. He is a challenging kind of person to reach. In this portion of Mark's gospel, we will see how Jesus transcends the barrier of this man's soundless world and reaches him.

The Necessity of Faith
This story continues the theme that Mark has been exploring—the Lord's training of the Twelve as He seeks to instruct them about who He truly is. It is instructive to realize that Jesus spent almost a third of His three-year ministry among Gentiles. This

fact is somewhat obscured by the emphasis on His ministry among the Jews. But if we look carefully at the map of the Lord's travels, we see that He has left the boundaries of Israel and entered into Gentile regions. He seeks to impart a sense of mission and ministry to the Gentiles in the minds of His Jewish disciples. Here we see Jesus traveling on the eastern side of the Sea of Galilee.

> *Then Jesus left the vicinity of Tyre and went through Sidon, down to the Sea of Galilee and into the region of the Decapolis. There some people brought to him a man who was deaf and could hardly talk, and they begged him to place his hand on the man.*
>
> *After he took him aside, away from the crowd, Jesus put his fingers into the man's ears. Then he spit and touched the man's tongue. He looked up to heaven and with a deep sigh said to him, "Ephphatha!" (which means, "Be opened!"). At this, the man's ears were opened, his tongue was loosened and he began to speak plainly.* (MARK 7:31–35)

Mark is careful to tell us that this incident took place in the area called the Decapolis, the ten Greek cities on the eastern side of the Sea of Galilee. And he points out that Jesus went into this region in a rather strange way. Instead of coming directly back into Galilee, He left Tyre and Sidon and went by a northern route through what is presently the country of Syria and continued down the eastern side of the Sea of Galilee into the southern part of that region. It would be much like traveling from San Francisco to Los Angeles, but instead of taking the direct route down the coast, you'd swing east and go by way of Reno and Las Vegas. Many scholars believe that this journey took about eight months.

So Jesus spent a great deal of time in the Gentile regions, ministering to non-Jews while teaching His Jewish disciples.

Every act of Jesus was a teaching act. There was a theme to everything He did. The theme of the healing of the man who was deaf and unable to speak is the absolute necessity of faith. Here is how Jesus dealt with the man.

First, Jesus took him aside privately. Deaf people have told me it is embarrassing to be deaf because no one can see your difficulty. If you are blind or lame, people see it and make allowances. But if you are deaf, no one can see it, and it is embarrassing to ask people to repeat their words slowly so you can read lips. Out of compassion for this man, Jesus led him away from the view of the multitude and dealt with him privately.

Next, Jesus did something unusual. He put His fingers into the man's ears. Then He spat on His fingers and touched the man's tongue. Next, looking into the heavens, He sighed. He did all this before He said the wonderful words "Be opened!" For years, I was baffled as to why He did this. But once, while studying this passage in preparation for a sermon on Mark, it came to me: Jesus was attempting to awaken and ignite this man's faith. In order to do so, He acted out what He wanted to convey to the man. After all, the man was deaf. How else could Jesus explain His intentions?

So Jesus put His fingers into the man's ears to indicate to the man that He intended to heal the man's ears. Then He moistened His finger and touched the man's tongue to indicate that He was going to heal the tongue, so that words would flow freely from it.

Then He looked up into heaven to indicate that the power for this act of healing would come from none other than God. And He sighed, not so much a sound as it was an exhalation, designed to convey to the man that by the invisible agency of God's power he would be made well.

When Jesus saw the response in the man's eyes—a look of trusting faith—He said *Ephphatha,* an Aramaic word (remembered, no doubt, by Peter, an eyewitness). The word means "be opened." The man's response was immediate: he suddenly began to hear and speak. That is amazing, for those who recover their hearing after a long period of silence usually cannot speak but must learn how.

This was Jesus' way of demonstrating, to us and to the disciples who were watching, that faith is a necessary ingredient to receiving anything from God. Faith is believing in the activity of an invisible God, trusting that He is ready and able to work in your life, even though you cannot see Him. Jesus awakened the faith of this man, so that he was able to believe in the invisible.

Seeing Beyond the Miracle

After He had healed the man, Jesus immediately took steps to prevent the abuse of this miracle. Mark writes:

> *Jesus commanded them not to tell anyone. But the more he did so, the more they kept talking about it. People were overwhelmed with amazement. "He has done everything well," they said. "He even makes the deaf hear and the mute speak."* (MARK 7:36–37)

Up to this point, Jesus has been dealing only with this man. But now He turns and speaks to the crowd, commanding the people not to spread the news of this healing. The Greek verb tense indicates that He kept telling them repeatedly, "Don't tell anyone! Don't tell anyone!" And the more He tells them to keep quiet, the more zealously they keep proclaiming it. The reason Jesus tried, on this and on other occasions, to keep people from spreading news of a healing was that He wanted to prevent the wrong emphasis, an emphasis on sensationalism, from taking hold. He did not want to become known as a mere wonder worker.

It is important to recognize an important difference between the attitude of the crowd and the attitude of the man who was healed. The crowd and the man had faith, but different kinds of faith, operating on different levels. The crowd believed in the wonder-working power of Jesus, and their eyes could see no further than the miracle. But the man had a different order of faith. He was not focused on a miracle but on the God who acts. That is where this man's faith rested, and that is where our faith should rest as well.

The crowd focused on what God did; the man focused on who God is. The crowd spread the news of an incredible event; the man was a witness to the reality of an awesome God. It is interesting to note that Jesus never tells the man not to speak of what has happened; He gives that command to the crowd. Evidently Jesus felt that it was safe to allow the man to be a witness, but He knew that it was not safe to allow the crowd to publicize what had happened. Only when your focus is on who God is, not what God does, are you qualified to be His witness.

Two Similar Miracles, Two Different Meanings

The account moves on into Mark 8. Ignore the break between Mark 7 and Mark 8; the chapter breaks were added centuries after these gospels were written, and they often come at the wrong place. The story of another mass feeding (the first was in Mark 6) logically follows the healing we saw at the end of Mark 7. These stories are connected by a single theme, and there should not be a break at this point. Mark writes:

> *During those days another large crowd gathered. Since they had nothing to eat, Jesus called his disciples to him and said, "I have compassion for these people; they have already been with me three days and have nothing to eat. If I send them home hungry, they will collapse on the way, because some of them have come a long distance."*
>
> *His disciples answered, "But where in this remote place can anyone get enough bread to feed them?"*
>
> *"How many loaves do you have?" Jesus asked.*
>
> *"Seven," they replied.*
>
> *He told the crowd to sit down on the ground. When he had taken the seven loaves and given thanks, he broke them and gave them to his disciples to set before the people, and they did so. They had a few small fish as well; he gave thanks for them also and told the disciples to distribute them. The people ate and were satisfied. Afterward the disciples picked up seven basketfuls of broken pieces that were left over. About four thousand men were present. And having sent them away, he got into the boat with his disciples and went to the region of Dalmanutha.* (MARK 8:1–10)

There are similarities between this account and that of the feeding of the five thousand in Mark 6. Despite the similarities, this is a different account. In Mark 6 the feeding involved five thousand people and took place in the Jewish area of Galilee; this account involved the feeding of four thousand people, and it took place in a non-Jewish region. Although some commentators have tried to assert that these are two different versions of the same event, Matthew and Mark want us to understand that they are two separate events. These two feedings were teaching events that Jesus used in the lives of His disciples, and each event had a different lesson to teach. Jesus, as we will see a bit later, refers to the two different events as having significance in the lives of His apostles.

Notice, first, the similarities of these two feedings. Bread and fish were the foods used in both cases, and our Lord multiplied them when they were brought to Him. Why did He repeat this miracle? Perhaps part of the answer is that He was doing with the Gentiles what He had also done among the Jews. Why? So the disciples would see that God's plan for the salvation of the Jews was also God's plan for the salvation of the Gentiles.

But Mark also makes it clear that the Lord's primary motivation was a simple and obvious one: His compassion for needy people. These people had been with Him for three days without any food. They had followed Him because they wanted to see Him perform miracles. Just as He knew would happen, the fast-spreading news of the healings brought people streaming out of the cities. They had come to witness a sensation, a wonder worker, a miracle man. For three days they had pursued Him in hope of seeing a miracle. He had probably taught them during this time, but the people were not content with hearing Him teach. It was a miracle they wanted.

Finally, after three days, they knew they had to return home. But Jesus was unwilling to send them away hungry. He was also unwilling to do any more miracles that would divert attention from His real message. So, finally, He decided to meet their physical need, and in the process, perform a miracle with a message— a teaching miracle that would instruct His disciples in several all-important truths. These are truths we need to learn as well.

First lesson: He wanted them to learn to begin with what they had. When you want God to act, do not wait for God to do everything. He expects us to be involved in the work He does. We are to be in partnership with Him. So we must start with what we have. When Jesus said He was going to feed the crowd and the disciples asked how He was going to feed all those people in the desert, He answered their question with a question: "How many loaves do you have?" They checked around and answered, "Seven." Jesus said, "That will do. Whatever you have to start with, turn it over for God's use. Just start with what you have."

Many of us want God to do a great work in our lives, and it is right to want that. He can do works in us and through us that we cannot do of ourselves. But we can do what we can do. We can begin with who we are and what we have. We can bring the bread, but He must multiply it. We can fill the jars with water, but He must turn it into wine. We must begin with what we have, and then He will take it and turn it into a miraculous, multiplied blessing for many.

At Peninsula Bible Church, where I have served as pastor, we practiced a biblical approach to church fellowship that came to be called Body Life. I later wrote a book called *Body Life,* in which I described this vital, warm, unified, loving form of Christian fellowship. People would hear about what was happening in our church or they would read the book, and then they would come to me and ask, "What is the secret formula for Body Life? How can I take this concept to my church and instantly get our pastor, our elders, our church board, our congregation excited about it? What is the miraculous shortcut to bringing Body Life into our church?"

And the answer I always gave was this: there is no secret formula. There is no shortcut. There is only one way to produce Body Life in your church. Go home and start where you are, using only what you have. Start in your home. Call together a small group of people who feel as you do, and begin practicing

Body Life in a small-group Bible study or fellowship group. Keep meeting, and God will bless from that. When people take that advice and put it to the test, they find out that God takes their dedicated little group and multiplies it, just as He multiplied the loaves and fish.

Second lesson: Jesus wanted them to learn that the supply will always equal or exceed the demand. God will never stop giving as long as the need remains. Our translation says, "When he had taken the seven loaves and given thanks, he broke them," but the English translation does not accurately convey the full, rich sense of the Greek, which tells us that Jesus kept on breaking the bread. Standing in front of the crowd, He took the seven loaves and began to break them. He did not build up a great pile of bread, and another pile of fish, and then say, "Now take that and distribute it." He handed it out a little at a time, but instead of running out, He kept handing out more bread and more and more. The supply of bread seemed endless. Then came the fish. And the same thing happened! There was plenty of bread and fish to feed everyone, and extra besides. Yet there was no visible resource from which He drew.

This is a powerful lesson for our lives. God wants us to learn to trust Him and to believe that He will always provide for us, even when there is no visible resource at hand. He wants us to know that He will provide not merely the bare minimum but a superabundance in our lives.

Our human tendency is to translate the word "abundance" into dollar signs, and it is true that God is faithful to meet our economic needs. For example, I can testify that every year at Peninsula Bible Church, we would total up the congregation's giving toward our various ministries, and we would always find that we had just enough to meet our needs, plus an extra hundred dollars or so. We never had a huge surplus. It was miraculous enough that we could always see God's hand at work, but never such an excess that we would begin to focus on God's works instead of on God. That is true abundance.

The abundance that God wants to bring into your life may have nothing to do with money. His goal is to meet our needs— our true, deep, eternal needs, not just our temporal wants. We must be open to allowing Him to work in any way He chooses, producing whatever result He deems most beneficial to our faith, maturity, and Christlike character.

Third lesson: Jesus wanted them to learn that spiritual bread is far more important than physical bread. All of the Lord's miracles were performed on the physical level, but they were designed to change people at the spiritual level. He does not want people to focus on the merely physical. He wants His disciples to see beyond mere bread and fish and to see the profound and eternally important lesson He has for them. He is driving home the lesson of the centrality of the spiritual. We experience spiritual hunger as well as physical hunger, and spiritual bread feeds spiritual hunger. If we focus only on physical bread, we will surely die; if we seek the Bread of Life, we will live forever.

Jesus demonstrated this for us when He was tempted by the devil in the wilderness. His answer to Satan is instructive to us all: "Man does not live on bread alone" (Matthew 4:4; Luke 4:4). Whether white, whole wheat, rye, or pumpernickel, mere bread is not enough for your humanity. If all you seek in life is physical provision—food, home, car, luxuries, entertainment, pleasure—your humanity will shrivel up within you. You must feed the spirit, or it will die. And it is true, as Jesus told us, that many people are dead inside, even though they are outwardly, physically alive.

The lesson of the loaves and fish is clear. As He told the people, "Do not work for food that spoils, but for food that endures to eternal life, which the Son of Man will give you. . . . I am the bread that came down from heaven" (John 6:27, 41). If you want to keep your spirit strong, so that you are able to understand reality as it truly is, so that you can cope with the trials and temptations of life, then you must learn to feed on the Bread from heaven, the Lord Jesus Christ. You must learn to draw the strength you need from Him and to worship Him and rejoice in Him. You need this Bread every day.

Many times I have counseled people who were struggling with problems in their lives or in their marriage. As we have talked, it has become clear that their problems were rooted in their loss of spiritual perspective. As a result, they were looking at life out of focus. Lacking God's perspective on their problems, they could not understand the problems in their relationships or their lives. As we talked together, they often began to see this spiritual lack in their lives. By praying, renewing their minds through the study of God's Word, and recommitting to drawing daily strength from Jesus Christ, they began to experience healing and forgiveness. Occasionally time would pass and they would return, saying, "I don't know what went wrong. I'm back in the same mess again." And more often than not, the problem was that they had drifted away from prayer, the Bible, and daily reliance on Christ. You cannot keep your spirit strong if you do not feed it. That is the lesson of this account. That is the Lord's lesson for His disciples, and for you and me.

Fourth lesson: Jesus wanted them to learn that God's resources are all-sufficient. This lesson is suggested by the intriguing fact that seven large baskets of food were left over. After the feeding of the five thousand in Mark 6, twelve baskets were left over. As we have discussed, twelve is the number used in Scripture to symbolize the twelve tribes of Israel. On that previous occasion, our Lord was telling the disciples that the lesson of the feeding of the five thousand, which took place in Israel and produced twelve extra baskets of food, was a truth that applied to Israel. But on this occasion, which took place in the Gentile region and produced seven extra baskets of food, Jesus had a new lesson to teach His disciples. Seven is the number of completeness and perfection; it always implies the full manifestation of God. This is why the number seven appears so often in the book of Revelation, for there God manifests Himself and the completion of His plan before all of creation.

Jesus is telling His disciples, "If you want to know God to the fullest, in all of His completeness, then talk to Him through prayer. Listen to Him by feeding daily on His Word. Feed on the Bread of Life."

Lessons Unlearned

Four lessons have emerged from the feeding of the four thousand. First, begin with what you have. Second, God's supply will always equal or exceed your demands. Third, spiritual bread is far more important than physical bread. Fourth, God's resources are all-sufficient.

Did the disciples learn these lessons? Unfortunately they didn't. And we can hardly judge them, for they are so much like us. Who among us can say that we have truly mastered these lessons? You and I are in the same boat with those disciples and their faltering faith and slow understanding. Mark goes on to tell us how these disciples failed to grasp the lessons Jesus tried so patiently to teach them.

> *He got into the boat with his disciples and went to the region of Dalmanutha.*
>
> *The Pharisees came and began to question Jesus. To test him, they asked him for a sign from heaven. He sighed deeply and said, "Why does this generation ask for a miraculous sign? I tell you the truth, no sign will be given to it."*
>
> (MARK 8:10–11)

Dalmanutha is across the lake, on the western side, near the present city of Tiberias. There the Pharisees came to argue and oppose Jesus. This was an attack staged by spiritually blinded men. They demanded "a sign from heaven." Jesus had given them not one sign but hundreds. He had healed the blind, lame, deaf, and the demonized. This was not their first encounter with Jesus; they had seen the things He had done. But they were determined not to believe in Him. They came to Him dishonestly, as if they were eager to know more of His ministry, but Jesus knew their evil intentions.

It is true that the Old Testament says that any prophet must give a sign to the people to prove he is a prophet. We would be wise to remember this truth in our age—that those who claim to be prophets should be able to demonstrate some sign that they are from God. In the Old Testament the sign was that they could predict something that was going to happen in the near future, and it would be fulfilled exactly as predicted. Those whose predictions were not accurately fulfilled were not from God.

But our Lord refused to give any sign. Why? Because He knew these men. He knew their hardened hearts. Matthew adds:

> *He answered, "A wicked and adulterous generation asks for a miraculous sign! But none will be given it except the*

> *sign of the prophet Jonah. For as Jonah was three days and*
> *three nights in the belly of a huge fish, so the Son of Man will*
> *be three days and three nights in the heart of the earth."*
>
> (MATTHEW 12:39–40)

Jesus was telling these Pharisees that the only sign they would be given was the sign of the resurrection. Jesus refused to work a miracle in their presence. Leaving them in their blindness and stubborn unbelief, He departed. Mark writes:

> *Then he left them, got back into the boat and crossed to*
> *the other side.*
> *The disciples had forgotten to bring bread, except for one*
> *loaf they had with them in the boat. "Be careful," Jesus*
> *warned them. "Watch out for the yeast of the Pharisees and*
> *that of Herod."*
> *They discussed this with one another and said, "It is*
> *because we have no bread." (MARK 8:13–16)*

The disciples' reaction is baffling. Why would they say, "We have no bread," when Jesus said, "Watch out for the yeast of the Pharisees and that of Herod"? The only plausible explanation is that the disciples' discussion indicates the workings of a bad conscience. They had forgotten to buy bread, and they thought Jesus was rebuking them for that. The moment He mentioned leaven, which is a subject related to bread, they tie His words to their failure to bring enough bread for lunch. That is how dull and confused they were.

Jesus tried to warn His disciples against the willful spiritual blindness of the Pharisees because the disciples were at risk of the same blindness. He spoke in metaphors. The leaven or yeast of the Pharisees and the Herodians was a picture of evil teaching. Jesus was telling the disciples that the Pharisees' blindness was caused by their teachings, their beliefs. The same was true of Herod and his followers.

The Pharisees believed that God was interested only in what you do, in your religious rites and ceremonial observances. According to this view, what you are like inside—your attitudes, your relationships, your thoughts and intentions—makes no difference. This is the basis of legalism, the view that true religion consists of rigid adherence to rules and laws. That is what Jesus called "the yeast of the Pharisees."

And what was "the yeast . . . of Herod"? Herod was a weak-willed king who ordered the execution of John the Baptist to fulfill the whim of his evil and vengeful wife (Mark 6:19–29). When Herod was presented with the demand for John's death, he looked around him at all the nobles and army officers in the banquet hall. He thought about what these people would think of him if he didn't carry out his promise. He was interested in doing only what made him acceptable to others, not what would make him acceptable to God. That was the yeast of Herod. It dulled his spirit and blinded him to the truth.

After warning His disciples against the yeast of the Pharisees and of Herod, Jesus overheard their discussion, and He saw how they had missed His point. Mark records Jesus' response.

> *Aware of their discussion, Jesus asked them: "Why are you talking about having no bread? Do you still not see or understand? Are your hearts hardened? Do you have eyes but fail to see, and ears but fail to hear? And don't you remember? When I broke the five loaves for the five thousand, how many basketfuls of pieces did you pick up?"*

> *"Twelve," they replied.*
>
> *"And when I broke the seven loaves for the four thou-sand, how many basketfuls of pieces did you pick up?"*
> *They answered, "Seven."*
>
> *He said to them, "Do you still not understand?"*
>
> (MARK 8:17–21)

Jesus diagnoses the spiritual condition of His disciples. They have hardened hearts, spiritual blindness, and spiritual deafness. Notice that He cites both feeding miracles and makes it clear that a lesson was attached to each miracle—and still they don't understand. They are spiritually dull and dead inside. They have the spiritual blahs.

I once spoke with a young man, a graduate of a Christian college. He told me, "I've been a Christian for many years, but I don't feel fulfilled. Instead, I feel empty—blah. I've lost all interest in what God is doing, and I don't have any desire even to study the Bible anymore. What should I do?" I had been studying Mark 8 when I encountered this young man, so I followed the same steps with him that our Lord followed in this passage.

Use your mind. Jesus says, "Do you still not see or under-stand?" In other words, "Stop and think about where you are, about what is happening to you and why it happened. Analyze it. Read what the Bible has to say about it. That is what the mind is for. Study God's revelation to you. Use your mind."

Analyze the state of your heart. Jesus asks, "Are your hearts hardened?" In other words, "What is the condition of your heart? Are you dull inside, or do you still respond to the truth? If the heart does not respond to what the mind has understood, then it is because you have not really believed it. You may have recog-nized mentally that it is true, but you have not acted on it. You do not really believe God is going to do what He says." God's truth always moves us, grips us, and excites us—when we believe it. If we are not excited, if we do not feel a response of joy, it is because the mind has grasped it but the heart has not. So we must pray that the eyes of the heart might be enlightened.

Look beyond the obvious, beyond the visible. Jesus says, "Do you have eyes but fail to see, and ears but fail to hear?" As you read through the gospels, you see that Jesus said these words again and again to His disciples. Each time, He means the same thing: "Don't look at the events you are seeing and think that is all there is to it. Each healing, each miracle is a visual parable, a way of conveying spiritual truth. When you saw people being fed by loaves and fishes, this was much more than a quick, free meal. I was trying to teach you a profound truth. I was telling you that you have a deep spiritual need that must be fed daily. Don't be spiritually blind. Use your eyes to see beyond the physical to the spiritual."

Remember all that God has done for you. Jesus asks, "And don't you remember?" He calls these two feedings to their remembrance and urges them to rediscover the meaning of these events. Jesus calls us to remember as well. Hasn't God taught you His truth through your past circumstances? Do you not remember the times He has shown His love and caring for you through difficult times in your life? Remember those times now, and always remember that you are in the hands of a loving Father. Learn to lay hold of His truth for your life and *rejoice!*

The same question Jesus posed to His disciples so many years ago He now poses to you and to me: "Do you still not understand?"

fourteen

The Turning Point

➤ **Mark 8:22–33**

Jazz pianist George Shearing was blind from birth. The composer of more than three hundred pieces, including the jazz standard "Lullaby of Birdland," Shearing toured continually throughout his long career. He could often be found in busy downtown areas, navigating crowded sidewalks with his dark glasses and white cane. On one occasion, he was at a busy intersection at rush hour, waiting for help in crossing the street. Finally someone tapped him on the shoulder. What Shearing heard next was not an offer for help but a request. "Excuse me, sir," a stranger said to Shearing, "would you mind helping a blind man cross the street?"

Shearing was about to tell the other man that he too was blind. Then he thought, *Why not give it a go?* So Shearing said, "Certainly, my friend. Here, take my arm." The two men set off across the street together, the blind leading the blind. Shearing heard many unnerving sounds as they crossed the street—tires squealing, horns blaring, the angry voices of cab drivers—but they made it safely to the far curb. Later Shearing recalled the incident and said, "I'll never do it again, but I'm glad I did it once. It was the biggest thrill of my life!"

The next passage we come to in Mark's gospel introduces us to another blind man, one who is about to experience a greater thrill than blindly crossing an intersection at rush hour. This blind man was about to experience one of the strangest and most remarkable miracles Jesus ever performed.

A Two-Stage Miracle

The healing that Jesus performs in Mark 8:22–33 is the only miracle He ever performed in two stages. It is the only healing that involved a process instead of an immediate transformation. Mark is the only gospel writer who records this miracle for us, and for that reason this miracle is rather obscure. Nevertheless it is a significant miracle, and it has a direct bearing on the startling change in the message of Jesus that follows this incident. Here is how Mark records this two-stage miracle:

> They came to Bethsaida, and some people brought a blind man and begged Jesus to touch him. He took the blind man by the hand and led him outside the village. When he had spit on the man's eyes and put his hands on him, Jesus asked, "Do you see anything?"
>
> He looked up and said, "I see people; they look like trees walking around."
>
> Once more Jesus put his hands on the man's eyes. Then his eyes were opened, his sight was restored, and he saw everything clearly. Jesus sent him home, saying, "Don't go into the village." (MARK 8:22–26)

Two things are of particular interest in this account: the process our Lord followed in performing this healing and the prohibition He imposed on this man.

The process is unique, and this should not surprise us, because Jesus never did two miracles alike. We tend to do things by habit, by repetition, but Jesus was not that way. He always shaped His works to the situation at hand, and He always acted creatively and with originality. In a real sense, every act of Christ was a work of art.

This miracle is startling because Jesus did something that seems shockingly unhygienic to us: He spit on the man's eyes. This was one of three miracles that are recorded in which Jesus used His saliva to perform an act of healing. We saw something similar in our previous study, when Jesus spit on His fingers, then touched His fingers to a man's tongue in order to heal him and enable him to speak. And in John's gospel there is an account of the healing of the man born blind; there Jesus anointed the man's eyes with clay formed from spitting on the ground. But in this account, Jesus spits directly on the eyes of this blind man.

Many Bible commentators have wrestled with the question of why Jesus did this. William Barclay suggests that this was an accommodation to the superstitious belief of that day that human saliva had therapeutic qualities. Even in our day, when a person burns or cuts his finger, he will put the finger to his mouth to soothe it. Perhaps there is something to this explanation, but it doesn't explain fully what our Lord was doing.

My theory about Jesus' action is based on my observation that everything our Lord does has a symbolic meaning and significance. All of His miracles were parables in action, intended to teach some deeper truth. So, in this case, I would suggest that perhaps Jesus' act of spitting into the blind man's eyes is a metaphor to suggest the Word of God issuing from the mouth of God. This act may have been intended by our Lord to awaken the faith of a blind man who could feel but could not see. Through the application of saliva to his eyes, the man may have sensed that something was going to happen that would involve the creative power of the spoken Word of God.

The healing process Jesus used is also startling because of the incompleteness of the healing. Many commentators have puzzled over the two-stage process involved in this miracle. Some have even gone so far as to suggest that this incident reflects a weakening of Jesus' powers. They reason that the opposition had become so intense, the hostility against Him so fierce, that it now took a double dose of His healing power in order to accomplish the healing.

I cannot subscribe to this school of thought. Our Lord always had adequate power to deal with any situation because, as He so frequently pointed out, these works were not accomplished by His power. It was the power of God the Father at work in Him. And if there is one truth that Scripture makes clear from the beginning of the Old Testament to the end of the New, it is that nothing is impossible for God.

Some commentators have suggested that perhaps this was an unusually stubborn case of blindness. But that is another way of saying that Jesus' power (or the Father's power) was inadequate to deal with the situation. It is hard to see how Scripture allows such a view.

So it seems to me that this two-stage healing was a deliberate act, performed for the benefit of the disciples. Jesus was using this miracle to teach His disciples an important truth. This incident falls within a section of Mark that deals with our Lord's repeated attempts to instruct the disciples. I would suggest that He deliberately performs this healing in two steps because He wants the disciples to see that they are like this blind man—and so are we. We, like the disciples, need to have our eyes opened in two stages, as this blind man did. If we read it this way, it becomes clear that this is an apt introduction to what follows.

A Strange Prohibition

Before we continue, let's look briefly at the prohibition our Lord laid on this man:

> *Jesus sent him home, saying, "Don't go into the village."*
> (MARK 8:26)

The village Jesus spoke of was Bethsaida. Our Lord had already done many miracles there, but now He orders this man to stay out of Bethsaida. This is in line with what we have seen Jesus do many times before. Often, after He had healed someone, He said, "Don't say anything about what happened to you." He did not want to encourage a focus on the miraculous and sensational. He was never happy about the fascination of the crowds, who craved only miracles.

But notice that Jesus does not merely command this man not to talk about the miracle. He exerts an even stricter control. He will not even let the man go into the village, lest he do what so many others had done: disregard the Lord's wishes and tell everyone. So Jesus limits this man to keep a sensationalized story from spreading around the countryside.

Immediately after Jesus sends the healed man on his way with a command to stay out of the village, Mark records that a crucial exchange takes place between Jesus and His disciples, an exchange that again ends with a command to keep silent about Jesus. Mark writes:

> *Jesus and his disciples went on to the villages around Caesarea Philippi. On the way he asked them, "Who do people say I am?"*
> *They replied, "Some say John the Baptist; others say Elijah; and still others, one of the prophets."*

> *"But what about you?" he asked. "Who do you say I am?"*
> *Peter answered, "You are the Christ."*
> *Jesus warned them not to tell anyone about him.*
>
> (MARK 8:27–30)

It is important to note the location of this conversation. Mark carefully records that it took place on the way to Caesarea Philippi, in the northern part of the Holy Land, north of the Sea of Galilee, at the foot of Mount Hermon. It is evident that our Lord was on His way to Mount Hermon. He was deliberately choosing steps that would take Him toward the Mount of Transfiguration (we will witness the Transfiguration in a few verses). Jesus understood that this was about to happen. He knew He was to be transfigured before several of His closest disciples. This conversation, then, is closely linked with the coming transfiguration of Jesus on the mountaintop.

Mark records that Jesus asked two questions of the disciples. First, He asked how the people in general regarded Him. Second, He asked for the disciples' view of Him. The first question elicited the answer that some people thought Jesus was John the Baptist, risen from the dead. Others thought He was Elijah the prophet. (Some Old Testament passages predict the reappearance of Elijah before the great and terrible Day of the Lord. Orthodox Jewish ceremonies still include a chair for Elijah at the Passover feast.) Yet others thought He was one of the prophets, such as Jeremiah or Isaiah, or perhaps a new prophet of that great old line of Hebrew prophets. These speculations showed that the people held Jesus in high regard, for these were the great names of Jewish history. But never once is it recorded that the people had even the slightest inkling that Jesus was in fact the Messiah.

Before leaving this issue of the Lord's identity, we should understand that the Jewish people did not believe in reincarnation. No passage in the Scriptures teaches reincarnation. When people thought that Jesus might be John the Baptist or Elijah or one of the prophets, they were not suggesting anything like the Eastern or New Age belief in reincarnation, that is, returning to life in a new body or new form. They were suggesting resurrection, a literal return to life in one's body and form. I would suggest that reincarnation is one of the deceptive beliefs the apostle Paul talks about when he writes, "The Spirit clearly says that in later times some will abandon the faith and follow deceiving spirits and things taught by demons" (1 Timothy 4:1).

"Who Do You Say I Am?"

The second question Jesus asked His disciples was, "Who do *you* say I am?" That was the all-important question. Peter's reply is immediate and definite: "You are the Christ," that is, the Messiah ("Christ" is the Greek form of the Hebrew word "Messiah"). Some people think that Christ is Jesus' surname, like my surname is Stedman. But "Christ" is not a name; it is a title. Jesus is His name; Christ is His office. Whether in the Greek or Hebrew form, that title means "the Anointed One." In the Old Testament, two offices required anointing: the office of king and the office of priest. When Peter answered with the words, "You are the Christ," that is, the Anointed One, he meant, "You are the one whom God has anointed King. You are the one predicted of old who would come to rule over the people of God and over the nations of earth. You are the Priest who is coming, the Anointed One."

Matthew records that Jesus said immediately to Peter, "Blessed are you, Simon son of Jonah, for this was not revealed to you by man, but by my Father in heaven" (Matthew 16:17). That is, "You did not come to this by simply reasoning it out, by normal human methods. Rather, it was revealed to you by my Father who is in heaven." Our Lord recognized that these disciples were being taught by the Holy Spirit. As they heard the Scriptures, saw the things Jesus did, and heard what Jesus said, their eyes were being opened by the Spirit. This teaching ministry of the Spirit goes on in our lives.

It is instructive to compare this dialogue with the account in Mark 4 of the stilling of the storm. On that occasion, some eight months before the events we are examining now, Jesus stood in a boat amid a raging storm, and He commanded the wind and waves to be still. Instantly a great calm came over the whole lake. It wasn't a gradual subsiding of the wind and waves. It was sudden and total, as if a huge hand had pressed down on the water, turning giant, foaming waves to a smooth sea of glass. And the disciples said to each other, "Who is this? Even the wind and the waves obey him!" (Mark 4:41).

It was a question that needed to be answered. Jesus had used all the events between the calming of the storm and this moment as teaching events to instruct the disciples as to His true identity. Now came the test. So Jesus put the question to them: "Who do *you* say I am?" Peter's answer was bold and clear: "You are not Elijah, or Jeremiah, or John the Baptist. You are not a lesser prophet. You are none other than the Christ. You are the one we have been looking for." Peter expressed the faith that was in all the disciples' hearts.

This was what Jesus wanted them to know. He had been working with them toward this end. He knew they needed to come to this knowledge, and all He had done up to this point had been designed to lead them to this understanding of His true identity as the Anointed One of God.

But now, having established that they truly do know who He is, Jesus does a strange thing. Mark tells us that He "warned" them. He commanded them sternly and in no uncertain terms that they were to tell no one about it. Isn't that strange? Wouldn't you think that Jesus would want them to tell everyone about Him? Wouldn't you expect Him to say, "Now that you know who I am, I am sending you out again. Go into every village and hamlet in Galilee and tell the people who I am." But Jesus does the opposite. "I warn you," He says, "don't you dare tell this to anyone!"

This is one of the puzzling developments in Jesus' ministry. And yet we can see why He did this, in the light of the story of the blind man He had healed a short time earlier. This is the first touch, which opened their eyes to a part of the truth. The disciples saw Jesus, but not clearly. They saw Him as the blind man had seen other people, as if He were a walking tree. They saw His greatness and His glory, but they did not understand the secret and the meaning of it. So they still required the second touch, and this is what our Lord goes on to give.

A Second Touch

The disciples knew that Jesus was the Christ, but they still had a deep misunderstanding of what the kingdom of God was like. They still did not even begin to understand how He was going to accomplish the work of the Anointed One. They were in awe of Jesus, but they still didn't comprehend Him. They were able to see Him, but dimly, vaguely, not clearly. So, just as Jesus gave a second touch to complete the healing of the blind man, He also gives a second touch to the disciples, so that their spiritual eyes will be fully open and able to see. Mark records:

> *He then began to teach them that the Son of Man must suffer many things and be rejected by the elders, chief priests*

and teachers of the law, and that he must be killed and after three days rise again. He spoke plainly about this, and Peter took him aside and began to rebuke him.

But when Jesus turned and looked at his disciples, he rebuked Peter. "Get behind me, Satan!" he said. "You do not have in mind the things of God, but the things of men."

(MARK 8:31–33)

Remember how the Lord commended Peter for saying, "You are the Christ." Then Jesus told the disciples that He would suffer and die, and Peter began to argue with Jesus. I'm sure Peter expected to be commended for taking a stand in defense of the Lord's life. Now Jesus not only had no word of commendation; He had a word of condemnation. "Get behind me, Satan!" said Jesus. "You do not have in mind the things of God, but the things of men."

The things of God are strange in the eyes of people. The disciples thought that everything Jesus had described to them—His suffering and death that were to come—were not merely strange but inconceivable. Jesus had commanded the wind and waves. He had healed many and cast out demons. He had fed the five thousand and the four thousand in a miraculous way. How could any human authorities capture Him, make Him suffer, and take His life from Him? Unthinkable!

Matthew and Mark specifically tell us that at this point in His ministry Jesus began to teach His disciples about the cross. He had hinted at it before, and Jesus knew from the beginning that He had come to die. In John's gospel, we see that even in His earliest ministry in Jerusalem, Jesus said to the Jewish leaders, "Destroy this temple, and I will raise it again in three days" (John 2:19). He had said to Nicodemus, who came to Him by night, "Just as Moses lifted up the snake in the desert, so the Son of Man must be lifted up" (John 3:14). Earlier in Mark's gospel, He compared Himself with a bridegroom who would be taken away and killed (see Mark 2:19–20). But these allusions to His approaching death were in the form of riddles, and the disciples did not understand them.

But now, Mark records, Jesus "began to teach them that the Son of Man must suffer many things and . . . be killed and after three days rise again. He spoke plainly about this." The tense of the Greek verb in Mark 8:32 suggests that He continued speaking plainly about these things. It is likely that He taught them over the course of several days. He plainly foretold His suffering and death. He plainly named the enemies they would face when they came to Jerusalem—the chief priests, the scribes, the Pharisees. And He plainly described what they would do to Him. Other accounts tell us that He detailed for them the floggings, beatings, and rejection that would take place. He put away parables and metaphors, and He plainly told them what was going to happen.

I do not think Peter's rebuke of the Lord was an immediate reaction. I suspect that Jesus taught the disciples for several days about His suffering and death, and Peter listened to this day by day until finally he could no longer stand it. Speaking for all the disciples, Peter took Jesus aside and rebuked Him. Imagine—Peter rebuking Jesus! He said, "Lord, you mustn't talk this way! These terrible things will never happen to you, to God's Anointed One! Don't speak this way anymore."

Matthew records that Peter said to Jesus, "Never, Lord! This shall never happen to you!" (Matthew 16:22). The sense of the Greek is that Peter literally says, "Spare yourself!" And isn't that the basic philosophy of the world we live in? Spare yourself. Nothing is more important than your interests, your safety, your comfort, your self.

When Peter uttered these words, Jesus responded with amazing harshness: "Get behind me, Satan! You are a stumbling block to me; you do not have in mind the things of God, but the things of men" (Matthew 16:23). Jesus' rebuke to Peter is withering in its directness and bluntness. Jesus is saying, "Get behind me, Satan! I recognize that voice. It came to me in the temptation in the wilderness: 'There's another way to get all that God wants for you. Think of yourself first. Spare yourself.' That is a sly attempt to divert me from my mission, but it won't work, so go!"

The Elements of the Cross

The disciples could not understand what lay ahead of their Lord. They could not understand that the cross is the glory of the Christian gospel. To them, the cross meant defeat. But Christ knew that the cross was the door to victory. That is why Paul, in Galatians 6, describes the cross as the one thing in all the world that he would "boast" of:

> *May I never boast except in the cross of our Lord Jesus Christ, through which the world has been crucified to me, and I to the world.* (GALATIANS 6:14)

Take the cross out of Christianity, and Christianity collapses. It is the cross that makes Christianity Christian. You cannot preach Christ without preaching the cross. There are three elements of the word of the cross. These three elements are found in Mark's gospel, and they are also found throughout the other gospels and the New Testament letters.

The first element of the way of the cross is the end of human self-sufficiency. How the world hates this aspect of the message of the cross! The world is in love with the self. Books, magazines, and talk shows extol the importance of self-fulfillment, self-gratification, and self-deification. There is even a magazine on the newsstands called *Self*. The self is the god of this age, and anyone who preaches the end of self-sufficiency preaches what this fallen world considers blasphemy. This age will have nothing to do with the cross or with the crucifixion of selfish desires and ambition. So this world rejects the word of the cross.

The message of the cross is that you and I can do nothing to save ourselves. Jesus did it all on the cross. Yet we have a hard time accepting that fact. Somehow there lingers within us the sense that we must contribute to our salvation, we must offer to God something that He can use, we must somehow make God a debtor to us. But the cross cancels out all human vanity and ego. We can add nothing to the cross or to our salvation. God owes us nothing; we owe Him everything.

The second element of the way of the cross is the necessity of pain, suffering, blood, and death. We do not like to hear that. It is a distasteful subject, not only because we are squeamish about such things, but because it reminds us that our sin caused His pain and death. Our sin caused the death of Jesus, and that is something we do not enjoy being reminded of.

Sometimes I hear Christians say, "I don't like to sing those old hymns that talk about how vile and sinful I am. I don't like to sing 'Amazing Grace,' because it talks about the grace 'that saved a wretch like me.' I don't like to think of myself as a wretch! I like to think of myself as a good person." The cross rebukes our foolish pride and reminds us that our sin is a horror to God, a stain on the universe—something so terrible and disgusting that it cost the Son of God incalculable suffering and torture and a cruel and ghastly death. The way of the cross always causes pain, and ultimately that brings us to the end of ourselves.

Jesus put it this way: "What is highly valued among men is detestable in God's sight" (Luke 16:15). What is highly valued in the world? Prestige, status, power, success, wealth, influence, fame, pleasure, comfort, security. These things, Jesus says, are an abomination in the sight of God. His standard of values is different. The cross is the most radical idea ever introduced in the world. We will never understand Christianity until we have understood the cross. Like the disciples, we have never seen Jesus until we have seen Him as one whose footsteps lead inexorably toward the cross. So our Lord begins to touch their eyes again that they might see Him as He really is—the suffering and soon-to-be-crucified Messiah.

The third element of the way of the cross is the reality of the resurrection. Isn't it strange that the disciples heard Him speak of His death on the cross, yet they failed to hear Him say that He would rise again? It never dawned on them what that meant. They seemed to be stuck at the cross and could never look beyond it to the empty tomb. Jesus predicted His resurrection as surely as He predicted His death. Yet the disciples could never understand what He was trying to teach them. They would not understand the resurrection until after it happened.

Resurrection—that is what we all truly want, what we long for and dream of. But we need a second touch in order to fully take hold of the reality of the resurrection. Jesus said there would be two stages to entering into the reality of the resurrection.

First stage: "Come to me, all you who are weary and burdened, and I will give you rest" (Matthew 11:28). There you learn who Jesus is, in the fullness of His power to give rest to a struggling, weary, laden heart. But that is not all. There is a second touch you must receive.

Second stage: "Take my yoke upon you and learn from me, for I am gentle and humble in heart." That is, like Christ, we set aside all prestige, pride, and status, seeking to live out His genuine humility and gentleness—"and you will find rest for your souls" (Matthew 11:29).

Here are the two stages of entering into resurrection living, and they are pictured for us in a beautiful metaphor in the two-step healing of the blind man. Knowing that Jesus is the Christ, the Anointed One of God, is only the first step. Then we must be brought into a deeper, clearer understanding of who He is and what it means to have, growing within us, the character of the Servant who rules, the Ruler who serves.

This account brings us to the turning point in the book of Mark, the place where the message of Jesus takes a new direction. Up to this point, Jesus has been portrayed for us as a servant of humankind. Up to this point, we have caught only brief glimpses of His true identity, although those glimpses are etched in our minds as a lightning flash etches a landscape onto our dazzled retinas. This Servant, it seems, has the power to command the wind and waves, forcing us to ask, along with the awestruck disciples, "Who is this? Even the wind and the waves obey him!"

But now, at this halfway point in the teaching of this book, Jesus begins to reveal Himself plainly to His disciples. He is not only the Servant who rules; He is the Ruler who serves, the anointed Priest-King of God who has come not to take His place on a throne in Jerusalem but to be nailed to a cross of shame outside the city walls. The Ruler has come to serve by suffering and dying for us all.

It is a message the disciples find impossible to accept. Yet it is the central truth of the gospel.

This shift in Jesus' instruction of His disciples is the turning point in our study, just as it is the turning point of the gospel of Mark. If we truly take hold of the truth that Jesus is teaching us, then I believe it will be the turning point of our lives as well.

Notes

Chapter 3: A Day in the Life of Jesus

1. J. T. Fisher and L. S. Hawley, *A Few Buttons Missing* (Philadelphia: Lippincott, 1951), 273.

Chapter 4: The Healer of Hurts

1. William Barclay, *The Gospel of Mark* (Philadelphia: Westminster John Knox Press, 1991).

Chapter 11: Who Is This?

1. Randy Bishop, "A Fire Worshiper Meets Jesus," *Christian Reader,* May/June 2000, electronically retrieved at http://www.christianitytoday.com/cr/2000/003/4.33.html.

Note to Reader

The publisher invites you to share your response to the message of this book by writing Discovery House Publishers, Box 3566, Grand Rapids, MI 49501, USA. For information about other Discovery House books, music, or videos, contact us at the same address or call 1-800-653-8333. Find us on the Internet at http://www.dhp.org/ or send e-mail to books@dhp.org.